Scott Foresman
Science

The Diamond Edition

PEARSON
Scott Foresman

Editorial Offices: Glenview, Illinois • Parsippany, New Jersey • New York, New York
Sales Offices: Boston, Massachusetts • Duluth, Georgia • Glenview, Illinois •
Coppell, Texas • Sacramento, California • Mesa, Arizona
www.pearsonsuccessnet.com

Series Authors

Dr. Timothy Cooney
*Professor of Earth Science and
Science Education*
University of Northern Iowa (UNI)
Cedar Falls, Iowa

Dr. Jim Cummins
Professor
Department of Curriculum,
Teaching, and Learning
The University of Toronto
Toronto, Canada

Dr. James Flood
*Distinguished Professor of
Literacy and Language*
School of Teacher Education
San Diego State University
San Diego, California

Barbara Kay Foots, M. Ed
Science Education Consultant
Houston, Texas

Dr. Shirley Gholston Key
*Associate Professor of Science
Education*
Instruction and Curriculum Leadership
Department
College of Education
University of Memphis
Memphis, Tennessee

Dr. M. Jenice Goldston
*Associate Professor of Science
Education*
Department of Elementary
Education Programs
University of Alabama
Tuscaloosa, Alabama

Dr. Diane Lapp
*Distinguished Professor of
Reading and Language Arts
in Teacher Education*
San Diego State University
San Diego, California

Sheryl A. Mercier
Classroom Teacher
Dunlap Elementary School
Dunlap, California

Karen L. Ostlund, Ph.D.
UTeach Specialist
College of Natural Sciences
The University of Texas at Austin
Austin, Texas

Dr. Nancy Romance
*Professor of Science Education
& Principal Investigator*
NSF/IERI Science IDEAS Project
Charles E. Schmidt College of
Science
Florida Atlantic University
Boca Raton, Florida

Dr. William Tate
*Chair and Professor of Education
and Applied Statistics*
Department of Education
Washington University
St. Louis, Missouri

Dr. Kathryn C. Thornton
*Former NASA Astronaut
Professor*
School of Engineering and
Applied Science
University of Virginia
Charlottesville, Virginia

Dr. Leon Ukens
Professor Emeritus
Department of Physics,
Astronomy, and Geosciences
Towson University
Towson, Maryland

Steve Weinberg
Consultant
Connecticut Center for
Advanced Technology
East Hartford, Connecticut

ISBN: 978-0-328-28959-2; 0-328-28959-0 (SVE); 978-0-328-30438-7;
0-328-30438-7 (A); 978-0-328-30439-4; 0-328-30439-5 (B); 978-0-328-30440-0;
0-328-30440-9 (C); 978-0-328-30441-7; 0-328-30441-7 (D)

3 4 5 6 7 8 9 10 V063 12 11 10 09 08

CC:N1

Consulting Author

Dr. Michael P. Klentschy
Superintendent
El Centro Elementary School District
El Centro, California

Science Content Consultants

Dr. Frederick W. Taylor
Senior Research Scientist
Institute for Geophysics
Jackson School of Geosciences
The University of Texas at Austin
Austin, Texas

Dr. Ruth E. Buskirk
Senior Lecturer
School of Biological Sciences
The University of Texas at Austin
Austin, Texas

Dr. Cliff Frohlich
Senior Research Scientist
Institute for Geophysics
Jackson School of Geosciences
The University of Texas at Austin
Austin, Texas

Brad Armosky
McDonald Observatory
The University of Texas at Austin
Austin, Texas

 Content Consultants

Adena Williams Loston, Ph.D.
Chief Education Officer
Office of the Chief Education Officer

Clifford W. Houston, Ph.D.
Deputy Chief Education Officer for Education Programs
Office of the Chief Education Officer

Frank C. Owens
Senior Policy Advisor
Office of the Chief Education Officer

Deborah Brown Biggs
Manager, Education Flight Projects Office
Space Operations Mission Directorate
Education Lead

Erika G. Vick
NASA Liaison to Pearson Scott Foresman
Education Flight Projects Office

William E. Anderson
Partnership Manager for Education
Aeronautics Research Mission
Directorate

Anita Krishnamurthi
Program Planning Specialist
Space Science Education and
Outreach Program

Bonnie J. McClain
Chief of Education
Exploration Systems Mission
Directorate

Diane Clayton Ph.D.
Program Scientist
Earth Science Education

Deborah Rivera
Strategic Alliances Manager
Office of Public Affairs
NASA Headquarters

Douglas D. Peterson
Public Affairs Officer,
Astronaut Office
Office of Public Affairs
NASA Johnson Space Center

Nicole Cloutier
Public Affairs Officer,
Astronaut Office
Office of Public Affairs
NASA Johnson Space Center

Reviewers

Dr. Maria Aida Alanis
Administrator
Austin ISD
Austin Texas

Melissa Barba
Teacher
Wesley Mathews Elementary
Miami, Florida

Dr. Marcelline Barron
Supervisor/K-12 Math
and Science
Fairfield Public Schools
Fairfield, Connecticut

Jane Bates
Teacher
Hickory Flat Elementary
Canton, Georgia

Denise Bizjack
Teacher
Dr. N. H. Jones Elementary
Ocala, Florida

Latanya D. Bragg
Teacher
Davis Magnet School
Jackson, Mississippi

Richard Burton
Teacher
George Buck Elementary
School 94
Indianapolis, Indiana

Dawn Cabrera
Teacher
E.W.F. Stirrup School
Miami, Florida

Barbara Calabro
Teacher
Compass Rose Foundation
Ft. Myers, Florida

Lucille Calvin
Teacher
Weddington Math &
Science School
Greenville, Mississippi

Patricia Carmichael
Teacher
Teasley Middle School
Canton, Georgia

Martha Cohn
Teacher
An Wang Middle School
Lowell, Massachusetts

Stu Danzinger
Supervisor
Community Consolidated
School District 59
Arlington Heights, Illinois

Esther Draper
Supervisor/Science Specialist
Belair Math Science
Magnet School
Pine Bluff, Arkansas

Sue Esser
Teacher
Loretto Elementary
Jacksonville, Florida

Dr. Richard Fairman
Teacher
Antioch University
Yellow Springs, Ohio

Joan Goldfarb
Teacher
Indialantic Elementary
Indialantic, Florida

Deborah Gomes
Teacher
A J Gomes Elementary
New Bedford, Massachusetts

Sandy Hobart
Teacher
Mims Elementary
Mims, Florida

Tom Hocker
Teacher/Science Coach
Boston Latin Academy
Dorchester, Massachusetts

Shelley Jaques
Science Supervisor
Moore Public Schools
Moore, Oklahoma

Marguerite W. Jones
Teacher
Spearman Elementary
Piedmont, South Carolina

Kelly Kenney
Teacher
Kansas City Missouri
School District
Kansas City, Missouri

Carol Kilbane
Teacher
Riverside Elementary School
Wichita, Kansas

Robert Kolenda
Teacher
Neshaminy School District
Langhorne, Pennsylvania

Karen Lynn Kruse
Teacher
St. Paul the Apostle
Yonkers, New York

Elizabeth Loures
Teacher
Point Fermin
Elementary School
San Pedro, California

Susan MacDougall
Teacher
Brick Community Primary
Learning Center
Brick, New Jersey

Jack Marine
Teacher
Raising Horizons Quest
Charter School
Philadelphia, Pennsylvania

Nicola Micozzi Jr.
Science Coordinator
Plymouth Public Schools
Plymouth, Massachusetts

Paula Monteiro
Teacher
A J Gomes Elementary
New Bedford, Massachusetts

Tracy Newallis
Teacher
Taper Avenue Elementary
San Pedro, California

Dr. Eugene Nicolo
Supervisor, Science K-12
Moorestown School District
Moorestown, New Jersey

Jeffrey Pastrak
School District of Philadelphia
Philadelphia, Pennsylvania

Helen Pedigo
Teacher
Mt. Carmel Elementary
Huntsville Alabama

Becky Peltonen
Teacher
Patterson Elementary School
Panama City, Florida

Sherri Pensler
Teacher/ESOL
Claude Pepper Elementary
Miami, Florida

Virginia Rogliano
Teacher
Bridgeview Elementary
South Charleston, West
Virginia

Debbie Sanders
Teacher
Thunderbolt Elementary
Orange Park, Florida

Grethel Santamarina
Teacher
E.W.F. Stirrup School
Miami, Florida

Migdalia Schneider
Teacher/Bilingual
Lindell School
Long Beach, New York

Susan Shelly
Teacher
Bonita Springs Elementary
Bonita Springs, Florida

Peggy Terry
Teacher
Madison District 151
South Holland, Illinois

Jane M. Thompson
Teacher
Emma Ward Elementary
Lawrenceburg, Kentucky

Martha Todd
Teacher
W. H. Rhodes Elementary
Milton, Florida

Renee Williams
Teacher
Central Elementary
Bloomfield, New Mexico

Myra Wood
Teacher
Madison Street Academy
Ocala, Florida

Marion Zampa
Teacher
Shawnee Mission
School District
Overland Park, Kansas

Science

See learning in a whole new light

How to Read Science xx

Science Process Skills xxii

Using Scientific Methods xxvi

Science Tools xxviii

Science Safety xxxii

Unit A Life Science

How do the different parts of a plant help it live and grow?

Chapter 1 • Plants and How They Grow

Build Background 2

Lab zone **Directed Inquiry Explore** How are plants alike and different? 4

How to Read Science Compare and Contrast . . 5

You Are There! 6

Lesson 1 • What are the main parts of a plant? 7

Lesson 2 • Why do plants need roots and stems? 10

Lesson 3 • How are plants grouped? 14

Lesson 4 • How do new plants grow? 18

Lesson 5 • How are plants from the past like today's plants? 22

Lab zone **Guided Inquiry Investigate** How fast do different kinds of seeds germinate? 26

Math in Science Elapsed Time From Seed to Fruit 28

Chapter 1 Review and Test Prep 30

NASA Career Plant Researcher 32

Chapter 2 • How Animals Live

Build Background 34

Directed Inquiry Explore How can you make a model of a backbone? 36

How to Read Science Sequence 37

You Are There! 38

Lesson 1 • How are animals grouped?. 39

Lesson 2 • How do animals grow and change? . . . 44

Lesson 3 • How do adaptations help animals? . . . 48

Lesson 4 • How are animals from the past like today's animals?. 54

Guided Inquiry Investigate What can you learn from an imprint? 58

Math in Science Comparing Speeds of Fish. 60

Chapter 2 Review and Test Prep. 62

Biography Paul Sereno: Expert Dinosaur Hunter 64

How do different animals live, grow, and change?

Unit A Life Science

How are ecosystems different from each other?

Chapter 3 • Where Plants and Animals Live

Build Background 66

Lab zone **Directed Inquiry Explore** In which soil do grass seeds grow best? 68

How to Read Science Main Idea and Details . 69

You Are There! 70

Lesson 1 • What are ecosystems? 71

Lesson 2 • Which ecosystems have few trees? 76

Lesson 3 • What are some forest ecosystems? 82

Lesson 4 • What are water ecosystems? 86

Lab zone **Guided Inquiry Investigate** How can you show that mold needs food? 90

Math in Science Comparing Data 92

Chapter 3 Review and Test Prep 94

NASA **Biography** Eric Stolen 96

Chapter 4 • Plants and Animals Living Together

How do plants and animals interact?

Build Background 98

Directed Inquiry Explore How do pillbugs stay safe? 100

How to Read Science Draw Conclusions . . . 101

You Are There! 102

Lesson 1 • How do living things interact? 103

Lesson 2 • How do living things get energy? 106

Lesson 3 • How do living things compete? 110

Lesson 4 • How do environments change? 114

Lesson 5 • What is a healthy environment for people? 120

Lesson 6 • How can people stay healthy? 124

Guided Inquiry Investigate What can happen in a place without predators? 128

Math in Science Health By The Numbers 130

Chapter 4 Review and Test Prep 132

NASA Moon Trees 134

Career Park Ranger 136

Unit A Test Talk 137

Unit A Wrap-Up 138

Full Inquiry Experiment How can a garden spider move across its web? 140

Science Fair Projects Germinating Seeds; Growing Mealworms; Selecting a Habitat; A Food Chain Model 144

ix

Unit B Earth Science

How does water change form?

How does weather follow patterns?

Chapter 5 • Water

Build Background 146

Lab zone Directed Inquiry Explore Where is Earth's water? 148

How to Read Science Cause and Effect . . . 149

You Are There! 150

Lesson 1 • Why is water important? 151

Lesson 2 • How do forms of water change? 156

Lab zone Guided Inquiry Investigate How can you make a model of the water cycle? 162

Math in Science Snowflake Geometry 164

Chapter 5 Review and Test Prep 166

Career Oceanographer 168

Chapter 6 • Weather

Build Background 170

Lab zone Directed Inquiry Explore How can you measure wind speed? 172

How to Read Science Make Inferences . . . 173

You Are There! 174

Lesson 1 • What makes up weather? 175

Lesson 2 • How are weather patterns different? . . . 180

Lab zone Guided Inquiry Investigate Can different amounts of carbon dioxide have different effects? . 184

Math in Science Comparing Temperatures 186

Chapter 6 Review and Test Prep 188

NASA Studying Clouds From Space 190

Career Air-Traffic Controller 192

Chapter 7 • Rocks and Soil

Build Background 194

Lab zone **Directed Inquiry Explore** What can you learn from rock layers? 196

How to Read Science
Compare and Contrast 197

You Are There! 198

Lesson 1 • How do rocks form? 199

Lesson 2 • What are minerals? 202

Lesson 3 • Why is soil important? 206

Lab zone **Guided Inquiry Investigate** How much water can soil hold? 210

Math in Science Living Soil 212

Chapter 7 Review and Test Prep 214

NASA Biography Dr. Elissa R. Levine 216

Why are rocks and soil important resources?

Unit B Earth Science

How do forces cause changes on Earth's surface?

Chapter 8 • Changes on Earth

Build Background 218

Directed Inquiry **Explore** How do some mountains form? 220

How to Read Science **Sequence** 221

You Are There! 222

Lesson 1 • What are Earth's layers? 223

Lesson 2 • What are volcanoes and earthquakes? . . 226

Lesson 3 • What are weathering and erosion? 230

Guided Inquiry **Investigate** How can you observe erosion? 234

Math in Science Measuring an Earthquake 236

Chapter 8 Review and Test Prep 238

NASA **Biography** Jean Dickey 240

Chapter 9 • Natural Resources

Build Background 242

Directed Inquiry Explore How can you classify resources? 244

How to Read Science
Compare and Contrast 245

You Are There! 246

Lesson 1 • What are resources? 247

Lesson 2 • How can we protect our resources? 250

Lesson 3 • What are ways to use resources again? . . 254

Guided Inquiry Investigate Where are some freshwater resources? 258

Math in Science Recycling 260

Chapter 9 Review and Test Prep 262

Career Recycling Plant Worker 264

Unit B Test Talk 265

Unit B Wrap-Up 266

Full Inquiry Experiment What settles first? . . . 268

Science Fair Projects: Predicting Weather; Comparing Soils; An Earthquake Model; Recycling 272

How can people use natural resources responsibly?

Unit C Physical Science

What are the properties of matter?

Chapter 10 • Matter and Its Properties

Build Background 274

Lab zone **Directed Inquiry Explore** Which material
has a surprising property? 276

How to Read Science Cause and Effect . . . 277

You Are There! 278

Lesson 1 • How can we describe matter? 279

Lesson 2 • How are properties of
matter measured? 284

Lab zone **Guided Inquiry Investigate** How can you
measure some physical properties of matter? 290

Math in Science Measuring Properties 292

Chapter 10 Review and Test Prep 294

NASA **Career** Chemist 296

What are physical and chemical changes in matter?

Chapter 11 • Changes in Matter

Build Background 298

Lab zone **Directed Inquiry Explore** How can matter
change? 300

How to Read Science Cause and Effect . . . 301

You Are There! 302

Lesson 1 • What are physical changes in matter? . . 303

Lesson 2 • What are some ways to
combine matter? 306

Lesson 3 • What are chemical changes in matter? . . 310

Lab zone **Guided Inquiry Investigate** How can
properties help you separate a mixture? 314

Math in Science A Closer Look at Mixtures 316

Chapter 11 Review and Test Prep 318

Career Firefighter 320

Chapter 12 • Forces and Motion

Build Background 322

Lab zone **Directed Inquiry Explore** How can you
describe motion? 324

How to Read Science Summarize 325

You Are There! 326

Lesson 1 • What happens when things
change position? 327

Lesson 2 • How does force affect motion? 332

Lesson 3 • How do simple machines affect work? . . 338

Lab zone **Guided Inquiry Investigate** How much force
will you use? 344

Math in Science Relating Speed, Distance, and Time. . 346

Chapter 12 Review and Test Prep 348

NASA Exercising in Space. 350

Biography The Wright Brothers 352

How do forces cause motion and get work done?

Unit C Physical Science

How does energy change form?

Chapter 13 • Energy

Build Background 354

Directed Inquiry Explore Can electricity
produce light and heat? 356

How to Read Science
Main Idea and Supporting Details 357

You Are There! 358

Lesson 1 • What is energy? 359

Lesson 2 • How does energy change form? 362

Lesson 3 • What is heat energy? 366

Lesson 4 • What is light energy? 370

Lesson 5 • What is electrical energy? 374

Guided Inquiry Investigate Do fresh
water ice and salt water ice melt the same way? . . 378

Math in Science Measuring Temperature 380

Chapter 13 Review and Test Prep 382

Career Electrical Engineer 384

Chapter 14 • Sound

Build Background 386

Lab zone **Directed Inquiry Explore** How can you see sound vibrations?. 388

How to Read Science Compare and Contrast 389

You Are There! 390

Lesson 1 • What causes sounds? 391

Lesson 2 • How does sound travel? 396

Lab zone **Guided Inquiry Investigate** How well does sound travel through different materials? 402

Math in Science Comparing Speeds of Sound 404

Chapter 14 Review and Test Prep 406

NASA **Biography** Clifton Horne 408

Unit C Test Talk 409

Unit C Wrap-Up 410

Lab zone **Full Inquiry Experiment** How does energy affect the distance a toy car travels?. 412

Science Fair Projects: Comparing Density; Separating Mixtures; Changing Potential to Kinetic Energy; Making Sounds 416

How does energy produce the sounds we hear?

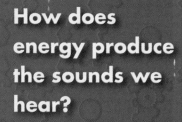

Unit D Space and Technology

Chapter 15 • Patterns in the Sky

What patterns do the Earth, Sun, Moon, and stars show?

Build Background 418

Lab zone Directed Inquiry Explore How do shadows change over time? 420

How to Read Science Sequence 421

You Are There! 422

Lesson 1 • What are some patterns that repeat every day? 423

Lesson 2 • What patterns repeat every year? 428

Lesson 3 • Why does the Moon's shape change?. . . 432

Lesson 4 • What are star patterns? 436

Lab zone Guided Inquiry Investigate When is the Big Dipper not the Big Dipper? 440

Math in Science Comparing Times of Sunrises and Sunsets 442

Chapter 15 Review and Test Prep 444

NASA The Hubble Space Telescope 446

Biography Galileo 448

Chapter 16 • The Solar System

How are the planets in the solar system alike and different?

Build Background 450

Lab zone Directed Inquiry Explore How can you make a distance model of the solar system? 452

How to Read Science Compare and Contrast 453

You Are There! 454

Lesson 1 • What are the parts of the solar system? . . 455

Lesson 2 • What are the planets? 458

Lab zone Guided Inquiry Investigate How can a planet's distance from the Sun affect its surface temperature? 466

Math in Science Patterns in Planets. 468

Chapter 16 Review and Test Prep 470

NASA **Career** Computer Engineer 472

Chapter 17 • Science in Our Lives

Build Background 474

Lab zone **Directed Inquiry Explore** Which transport
system works best? 476

How to Read Science Sequence 477

You Are There! 478

Lesson 1 • How does technology affect our lives? . . 479

Lesson 2 • What are some new technologies? 484

Lesson 3 • How does technology help us get energy?. 490

Lab zone **Guided Inquiry Investigate** How does a
GPS device find your location? 498

Math in Science Technology Through the Years 500

Chapter 17 Review and Test Prep 502

NASA **Career** Science Teacher 504

Unit D Test Talk 505

Unit D Wrap-Up 506

Lab zone **Full Inquiry Experiment** How does the speed
of a meteorite affect the crater it makes? 508

Discovery School **Science Fair Projects:** Observing Patterns of
Daylight; Planet-Size models; Inventing 512

Metric and Customary Measures EM1

Glossary EM2

Index EM7

Credits EM26

How does technology affect our lives?

How to Read Science

A page like the one below is found near the beginning of each chapter. It shows you how to use a reading skill that will help you understand what you read.

Before Reading

Before you read the chapter, read the Build Background page and think about how to answer the question. Recall what you already know as you answer the question. Work with a partner to make a list of what you already know. Then read the How to Read Science page.

Target Reading Skill
Each page has one target reading skill. The reading skill corresponds with a process skill in the Directed Inquiry activity on the facing page. The reading skill will be useful as you read science.

Real-World Connection
Each page has an example of something you might read. It also connects with the Directed Inquiry activity.

Graphic Organizer
A useful strategy for understanding anything you read is to make a graphic organizer. A graphic organizer can help you think about the information and how parts of it relate to each other. Each reading skill has a graphic organizer.

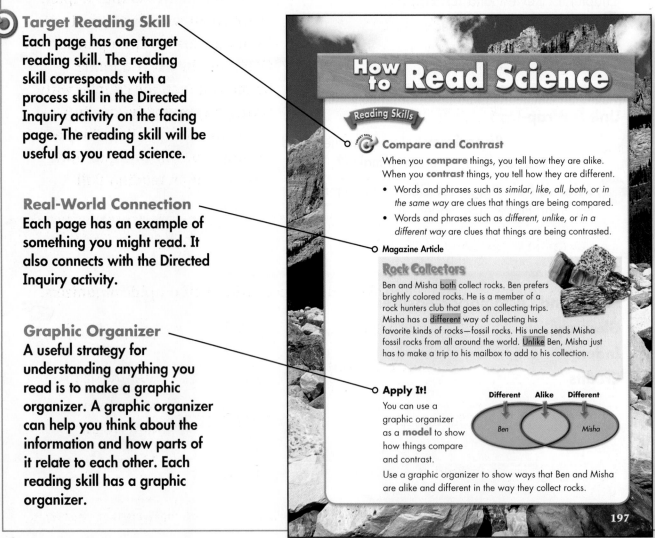

How to Read Science

Reading Skills

Compare and Contrast

When you **compare** things, you tell how they are alike. When you **contrast** things, you tell how they are different.

- Words and phrases such as *similar, like, all, both,* or *in the same way* are clues that things are being compared.
- Words and phrases such as *different, unlike,* or *in a different way* are clues that things are being contrasted.

Magazine Article

Rock Collectors

Ben and Misha both collect rocks. Ben prefers brightly colored rocks. He is a member of a rock hunters club that goes on collecting trips. Misha has a different way of collecting his favorite kinds of rocks—fossil rocks. His uncle sends Misha fossil rocks from all around the world. Unlike Ben, Misha just has to make a trip to his mailbox to add to his collection.

Apply It!

You can use a graphic organizer as a **model** to show how things compare and contrast.

Different   Alike   Different

Ben   Misha

Use a graphic organizer to show ways that Ben and Misha are alike and different in the way they collect rocks.

Properties of Minerals

Mineral	Color	Luster	Streak	Hardness
Mica Mica breaks into flaky pieces when struck.	black, gray, green, violet	pearly on surfaces	white	can be scratched with a knife
Molybdenite This mineral is one of the strongest and most commonly used heat-resistant metals.	silvery	metallic	bluish gray	can be scratched with a fingernail
Crocoite Much of this mineral comes from Australia.	reddish-orange	very shiny	orange-yellow	can be scratched with a coin

Another way to identify a mineral is to test its hardness. Some minerals, such as talc, are so soft you can scratch them with your fingernail. The hardest mineral is diamond. It can be scratched only by another diamond.

Some minerals can be identified by their appearance. Gold, for example, appears sometimes in nugget form. Other minerals can be identified by taste, smell, or touch.

1. **Checkpoint** What are ways to identify minerals?

2. **Compare and Contrast** How are rocks and minerals alike? How are they different? Use a graphic organizer to show your answer.

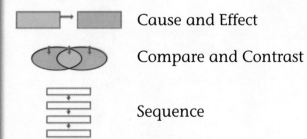

203

Process Skills

13. **Predict** Which would dry faster after it rains: a sandy beach or a grassy field? Give a reason for your answer.

14. **Model** Make a model or a drawing that shows the different layers of soil.

15. **Infer** You observe that a mineral sample can be scratched with a coin. What do you infer about the hardness of the mineral?

Compare and Contrast

16. Make a graphic organizer like the one below. Fill it in to compare and contrast sandy soil and clay soil.

Sandy soil — Both types of soil — Clay soil

Test Prep

Choose the letter that best completes the statement or answers the question.

17. All rocks contain
A loam.
B minerals.
C water.
D sediments.

18. In what rocks are fossils most often found?
F sedimentary
G igneous
H metamorphic
I all of the above

19. The layer of soil just below the topsoil is
A loam.
B decayed matter.
C rock.
D subsoil.

20. **Writing in Science**
Persuasive Write a letter to a member of a city council that discusses why rich farmland is valuable to everyone in the community.

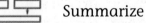

215

During Reading

As you read the lesson, use the Checkpoint to check your understanding. Some checkpoints ask you to use the target reading skill.

After Reading

After you have read the chapter, think about what you found out. Exchange ideas with a partner. Compare the list you made before you read the chapter with what you learned by reading it. Answer the questions in the Chapter Review. One question uses the target reading skill.

Graphic Organizers

These are the target reading skills that appear with their graphic organizers.

- Cause and Effect
- Compare and Contrast
- Sequence
- Predict
- Draw Conclusions
- Summarize
- Main Idea and Details
- Make Inferences

Science Process Skills

Investigating Weather

Scientists use process skills when they investigate places or events. You will use these skills when you do the activities in this book. Which process skills might scientists use when they investigate weather?

Observe

A scientist who studies weather observes many things. You use your senses too to find out about other objects, events, or living things.

Classify

Scientists classify clouds according to their properties. When you classify, you arrange or sort objects, events, or living things.

Estimate and Measure

Scientists estimate how much rain will fall. Then they use tools to measure how much rain fell.

Infer

Scientists infer what they think is happening during a storm, based on what they already know.

Predict

Scientists predict how weather will change. Then people know how to get ready for the change.

Make and Use Models

Scientists make and use models such as pictures and maps. Models are like real events in some ways, but are different in other ways.

Make Operational Definitions

Scientists can use what they know to make operational definitions about what they observe during a storm.

Science Process Skills

Form Questions and Hypotheses

Think of a statement that you can test to solve a problem or answer a question about storms or other kinds of weather.

Investigate and Experiment

As scientists observe storms, they investigate and experiment to test a hypothesis.

Identify and Control Variables

As scientists perform an experiment, they identify and control the variables so that they test only one thing at a time.

If you were a scientist, you might want to learn more about storms. What questions might you have about storms? How would you use process skills in your investigation?

Collect Data
Scientists collect data from their observations of weather. They put the data into charts or tables.

Interpret Data
Scientists use the information they collected to solve problems or answer questions.

Communicate
Scientists use words, pictures, charts, and graphs to share information about their investigation.

Using Scientific Methods for Science Inquiry

Scientists use scientific methods as they work. Scientific methods are organized ways to answer questions and solve problems. Scientific methods include the steps shown here. Scientists might not use all the steps. They might not use the steps in this order. You will use scientific methods when you do the **Full Inquiry** activity at the end of each unit. You also will use scientific methods when you do Science Fair Projects.

Ask a question.

You might have a question about something you observe.

What material is best for keeping heat in water?

State your hypothesis.

A hypothesis is a possible answer to your question.

If I wrap the jar in fake fur, then the water will stay warm the longest.

Identify and control variables.

Variables are things that can change. For a fair test, you choose just one variable to change. Keep all other variables the same.

Test other materials. Put the same amount of warm water in other jars that are the same size and shape.

Test your hypothesis.

Make a plan to test your hypothesis. Collect materials and tools. Then follow your plan.

Collect and record your data.

Keep good records of what you do and find out. Use tables and pictures to help.

Interpret your data.

Organize your notes and records to make them clear. Make diagrams, charts, or graphs to help.

State your conclusion.

Your conclusion is a decision you make based on your data. Communicate what you found out. Tell whether or not your data supported your hypothesis.

Fake fur kept the water warm longest. My data supported my hypothesis.

Go further.

Use what you learn. Think of new questions to test or better ways to do a test.

Ask a Question

State Your Hypothesis

Identify and Control Variables

Test Your Hypothesis

Collect and Record Your Data

Interpret Your Data

State Your Conclusion

Go Further

Science Tools

Scientists use many different kinds of tools. Tools can make objects appear larger. They can help you measure volume, temperature, length, distance, and mass. Tools can help you figure out amounts and analyze your data. Tools can also help you find the latest scientific information.

You should use **safety goggles** to protect your eyes.

You use a **thermometer** to measure temperature. Many thermometers have both Fahrenheit and Celsius scales. Scientists usually use only the Celsius scale.

You can use a **telescope** to help you see things that are very far away, such as stars and planets.

Binoculars make far-away objects appear larger, so you can see more of their details.

A **hand lens** doesn't enlarge things as much as a microscope does, but it is easier to carry.

Scientists use **rulers and metersticks** to measure length and distance.

A **balance** like this one can be used to measure mass.

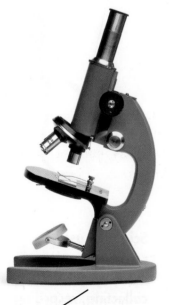

Microscopes use several lenses to make objects appear much larger, so you can see more detail.

Science Tools

Magnets can be used to test if an object is made of certain metals such as iron.

Pictures taken with a **camera** record what something looks like. You can compare pictures of the same object to show how the object might have changed.

A **graduated cylinder** can be used to measure volume, or the amount of space an object takes up.

You can figure amounts using a **calculator**.

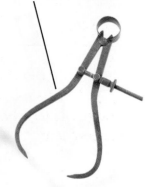

Calipers can be used to measure the width of an object.

Scientists use **computers** in many ways, such as collecting, recording, and analyzing data.

You can talk into a **sound recorder** to record information you want to remember.

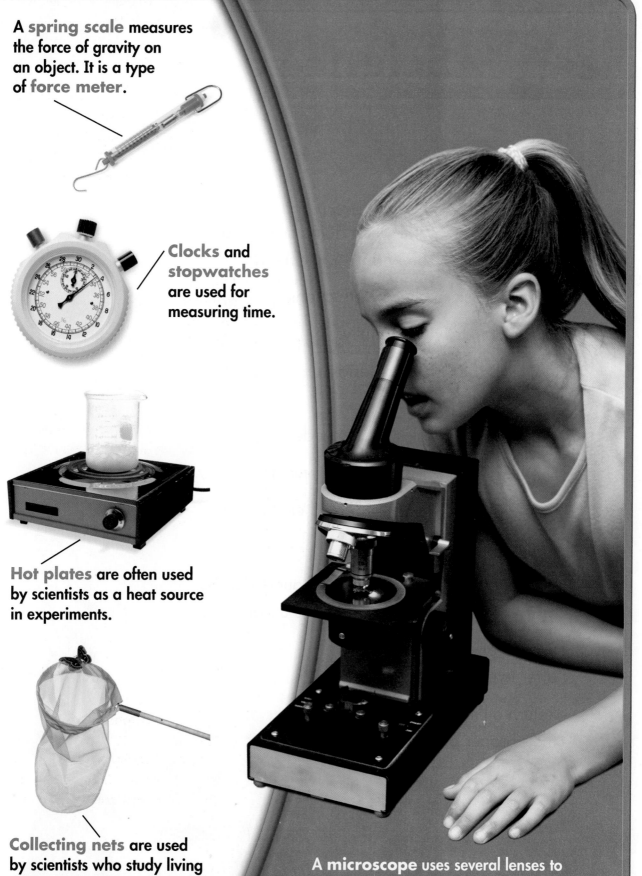

A **spring scale** measures the force of gravity on an object. It is a type of **force meter**.

Clocks and **stopwatches** are used for measuring time.

Hot plates are often used by scientists as a heat source in experiments.

Collecting nets are used by scientists who study living things. They are used to collect organisms.

A **microscope** uses several lenses to make objects appear much larger, so you can see more detail.

Safety in Science

You need to be careful when doing science activities. This page includes safety tips to remember:

- Listen to your teacher's instructions.

- Read each activity carefully.

- Never taste or smell materials unless your teacher tells you to.

- Wear safety goggles when needed.

- Handle scissors and other equipment carefully.

- Keep your work place neat and clean.

- Clean up spills immediately.

- Tell your teacher immediately about accidents or if you see something that looks unsafe.

- Wash your hands well after every activity.

- Return all materials to their proper places.

You Will Discover

- why all living things need water.
- how much water Earth has.
- how water changes phase.
- how water is cleaned.

Chapter 5
Water

online
Student Edition
pearsonsuccessnet.com

How does water change form?

wetland

water cycle

water vapor

evaporation

groundwater

146

Chapter 5 Vocabulary

. . . .

water vapor page 154

groundwater page 155

wetland page 155

evaporation page 157

condensation page 157

water cycle page 158

precipitation page 159

precipitation

condensation

147

Directed Inquiry

Explore Where is Earth's water?

What if all of Earth's water would fit in a bottle?

Materials

2 L plastic bottle filled with water

4 cups

dropper and masking tape

funnel and graduated cylinder (or measuring cup)

What to Do

Earth's Water	Amount of Water (total = 2200 mL)
Atmosphere (fresh water)	about $\frac{1}{2}$ drop
Lakes, rivers, streams (fresh water)	about 4 drops
Groundwater (fresh water)	13 mL
Icecaps and glaciers (fresh water)	47 mL
Oceans and seas (salt water)	2139 mL

1️⃣ Label the 4 cups.

2️⃣ Look at the chart. Find the amount of water shown for the atmosphere. Take out that amount of water from the bottle. Put it in the atmosphere cup.

Hold the bottle with both hands.

3️⃣ Repeat for the other places water is found. Use the graduated cylinder when needed.

4️⃣ Label the bottle *oceans and seas.*

Process Skills

Thinking about causes and effects can help you make **inferences.**

Explain Your Results

Infer Why should people use fresh water wisely?

Reading Skills

TARGET SKILL

Cause and Effect

A **cause** makes something happen. An **effect** is what happens. Science writers often use clue words and phrases such as *because, so, since,* and *as a result* to signal cause and effect. The following example will help you **infer** why people should use fresh water wisely.

Science Article

Clean Streams

Factories make things for people. They often use water that gets dirty. Dumping this water into streams can harm wildlife and our water supply. As a result, the government makes laws to reduce the harm done. These laws help keep our environment clean.

Apply It!

Make a graphic organizer like the one shown. Then use it to list three causes and an effect from the science article.

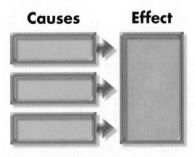

Causes   Effect

Bright sunlight gives way to rain clouds. Little splashes of water appear on the lake. Suddenly rain is pouring down all around you. Your face and clothes are quickly soaked. Too bad you don't have the waterproof feathers of a duck. Getting wet can be a bother, but what makes water so important?

Lesson 1

Why is water important?

You could go without sweets or TV if you had to. But you can't give up water. You could not live more than a few days without it.

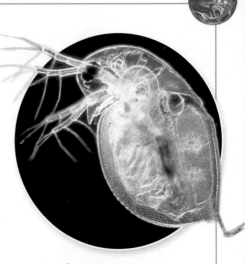

Daphnia are very tiny. This picture was taken through a microscope.

Living Things and Water

Living things from big trees to small snails need water to survive and grow. Green plants need water to make food. Fish and other animals need oxygen in water to breathe.

Water makes up about two-thirds of your body. Water is busy helping every part of your body. For example, water helps digest food into small particles. Water in your blood carries materials to every part of your body. Water also carries wastes away from every part.

Water helps keep your body at the correct temperature. What if the air temperature turns cold? Water in your body tends to hold onto its heat, keeping you warm. If your body heats up, you might sweat. The water in sweat carries heat away from your body.

Some organisms must spend their whole lives in water. Many of these creatures are very small. Daphnia, for example, are less than 1.5 mm long. Daphnia live mostly in ponds and lakes.

1. **✓Checkpoint** How does water help you live?

2. **Health in Science** Why is it important to drink water, especially after you exercise?

151

The Uses of Water

People use water in many ways. Lakes, rivers, and oceans supply us with fish and shellfish. Farmers use water to help make crops grow. Some of this water falls from the sky. But some flows through pipes to fields.

People use the power of moving water to make electricity. They build dams and power stations across rivers. Rushing water turns giant wheels inside turbines. Turbines help make electricity. This electricity can travel long distances through wires.

We also use water for transportation and enjoyment. Large ships carry goods from one place to another. Some people row on ponds or sail across oceans. Others go tubing, or swimming, or canoeing. People can have fun in the water.

Most plants take in water through their roots to grow.

1. ✓**Checkpoint** List three ways that people use water.

2. **Cause and Effect** What would happen if we did not protect our supply of fresh water?

Drinking

People need to drink water. All animals need water too. This impala slurps up a drink. The tiny bird on its horn will have some too.

Food

Water provides food. People get animals from the sea. Some fish live near the bottom of the sea. Others can be seen from boats. Boats bring back seaweed as well as fish. Seaweed is food for people and animals.

Crops and Farms

In many parts of the world, farmers irrigate land. They bring water to it. The water lets farmers grow crops in many places where no crops grew before. One third of water used in the U.S. is for irrigation.

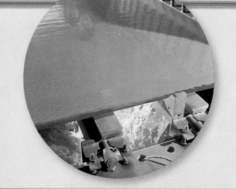

Industry

Factories use water in many different ways. Water is used to clean foods and the insides of buildings. It is used to make paper and steel. Most of the water used in manufacturing is later put back into rivers and streams.

Electricity

Water is used to make electricity. Moving water or steam can turn large turbines. Turbines are special engines that help make power. Electric power can be used for light, heat, and to run machines.

The Planet of Water

You could call Earth "the blue planet." That's because about three fourths, or 75 percent, of Earth's surface is covered with water.

Most of Earth's water is salty ocean water. Some of the salt in ocean water comes from rock on the ocean floor. Other salt is washed off the land into the oceans. The salt mixes with the water. You cannot drink, wash clothes, or water plants with ocean water. You cannot use this water to make products in factories.

Water is found in many places. Some water moves downward into the ground. Some is frozen into ice. Some water is found in the air as an invisible gas called **water vapor.** Clouds are made of water vapor that has changed to tiny drops of liquid water.

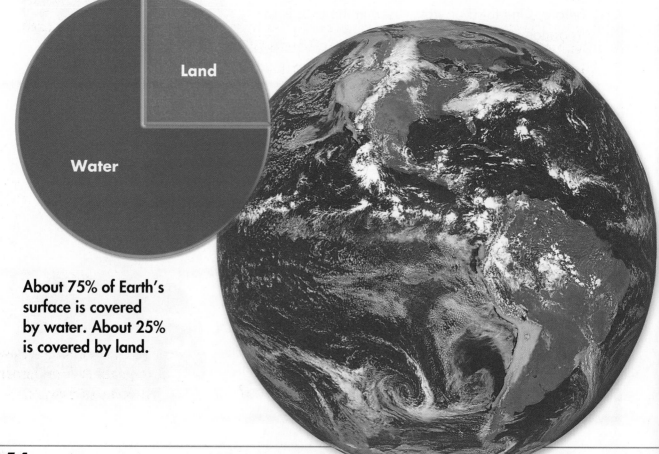

About 75% of Earth's surface is covered by water. About 25% is covered by land.

Fresh Water

There is little salt in fresh water. We need fresh water to drink. A very small amount of the water on Earth is fresh water. Most of this water is frozen as ice near the North and South Poles.

Many lakes, rivers, and streams supply fresh water. Streams run together to form rivers. Rivers can flow into and out of lakes.

Some of the fresh water we use comes from underground. Water seeps down slowly through the soil. It collects in spaces between underground rocks. This water is called **groundwater.** People dig wells to bring groundwater to the surface.

In some places, the top level of the groundwater is very close to Earth's surface. If water soaks the ground at least part of the year, the place is called a **wetland.**

Wetlands are homes for many animals. They also help prevent floods by soaking up extra water. Some water in wetlands seeps down through soil. This helps refill the groundwater supply.

A spring is a stream of groundwater that flows out of the ground.

Fresh water is frozen in huge chunks of ice. This iceberg is near Antarctica.

Small streams can flow together to form larger streams and rivers.

✓ Lesson Checkpoint

1. Why is fresh water important?
2. What are four sources of fresh water?
3. **Writing in Science** **Descriptive** In your **science journal**, write a paragraph about a time you spent near water. What did you see? What did you hear? What did you feel?

How Water Moves Around Earth

There is only a certain amount of water on Earth. It must be used again and again. The movement of water from Earth's surface into the air and back again is the **water cycle.** The water cycle gives us a constant supply of fresh water.

Water changes form or state as it moves through the water cycle. The Sun's energy and winds cause water to evaporate and become water vapor.

Rain is just one form of precipitation.

Precipitation can fall as snow.

Precipitation

Stream water flow

The arrows show some of the main paths water takes as it cycles through the environment.

Groundwater flow

Water vapor rises into cooler air, cools, and turns into water droplets or ice crystals. This process is called condensation. These water particles collect and form clouds.

When water particles in clouds grow in size and weight, they fall faster. Water that falls to Earth is called **precipitation.** Precipitation might be rain, snow, sleet, or hail.

Some precipitation seeps into the ground. There it becomes groundwater. Other precipitation falls onto streams, rivers, lakes, and oceans. Water that flows across Earth's surface is constantly moving downstream toward the ocean. A lot of ground water reaches the surface in lower areas where there are streams and rivers. This surface water evaporates. In this way, the water cycle continues all the time—everywhere.

Snowflakes can form when the temperature is below 0°C.

Condensation

Water vapor

Evaporation

1. ✓ **Checkpoint** Name the main steps in the water cycle.

2. **Cause and Effect** What kind of precipitation would occur if the temperature was above freezing?

Ways to Clean Water

People need clean water. Water may contain germs that make people sick. It may contain dirt or salt that can harm machines. These things can make the water taste and smell bad. The water that people use is cleaned to remove these things.

In some places, people get water from their own wells. They must filter the water to remove dirt and chemicals.

In cities, people do not need to clean their own water. The water for most cities is cleaned in one place. First, the water is sent through pipes to a water-treatment area. There, several things may happen.

This filter cleans only the water that comes out of this faucet.

This kind of filter cleans all the water that comes into this building.

Chemicals may be added to the water. Some chemicals kill germs. Others, such as fluoride, help make teeth strong.

In some treatment plants, the water is sprayed into the air. This makes the water taste and smell better. Often, the water is stored in big tanks for a while. Tiny pieces of dirt sink to the bottom of the tank. Finally, the water is pumped through a filter. Even more dirt is removed.

The water now is clean. It can be pumped all over the city. Homes and businesses will have clean, fresh water to use.

Map Fact

The city of Chicago has two of the largest water-cleaning plants in the world. These clean between one and two billion gallons of water a day. People who live in and around Chicago use this water.

A water-cleaning plant in Chicago

✔ Lesson Checkpoint

1. What properties of water allow the water cycle to take place?

2. Why must water be cleaned?

3. **Writing** in Science **Expository** Explain in your **science journal** what happens to the water in a puddle on a hot day. Include at least two steps of the water cycle.

Investigate How can you make a model of the water cycle?

Materials

ice cube

cup

resealable plastic bag

tape

What to Do

1 Put an ice cube in the cup.

2 Put the cup into the bag. Seal the bag.

3 Tape the bag to a sunny window. **Predict** what will happen over the next 3 days.

Process Skills

An **inference** about a future event is called a **prediction**.

More Lab zone **Activities** Take It to the Net pearsonsuccessnet.com

4 **Observe** the bag. Record what happens. Compare your results with your predictions.

Time	Predictions	Observations
After 2 hours		
Day 2		
Day 3		

Explain Your Results

1. Make a drawing. Show how the water from the ice cube moved to the bottom of the bag. Use arrows. Use these words as labels: *melting, evaporation,* and *condensation.*

2. **Infer** What do you think would happen if the entire bag was put in a freezer?

3. Identify the different forms in which water exists in the air. How does water change from one form to another?

Go Further

How do you think you could make the water cycle happen faster or slower in the bag? Design and conduct a scientific investigation to test your prediction. Keep a record in a journal.

Chapter 5 Review and Test Prep

Use Vocabulary

condensation (page 157)	**water cycle** (page 158)
evaporation (page 157)	**water vapor** (page 154)
groundwater (page 155)	**wetland** (page 155)
precipitation (page 159)	

Use the vocabulary word from the list above that best completes each sentence.

1. _____ happens when water changes into water vapor and rises into the air.

2. An area where water soaks the ground for at least part of the year is called a(n) _____.

3. The _____ moves water from Earth's surface into the air and back again.

4. When water evaporates, it turns into an invisible gas called _____.

5. Water that falls from clouds in the form of rain, snow, sleet, or ice is called _____.

6. _____ occurs when water vapor changes back into water droplets.

7. Fresh water found under the ground is _____.

Explain Concepts

8. Explain why all living things need water.

9. Describe where water is found on the Earth.

10. Why is most of Earth's water salt water?

11. Describe the changes that water goes through in the water cycle.

Process Skills

12. **Infer** Why is it important that poisonous materials do not leak into the ground?

13. **Predict** What might happen to a glass bottle if it is filled with water, capped tightly, and put in the freezer?

Cause and Effect

14. Make a graphic organizer like the one shown below. Fill in the correct effect.

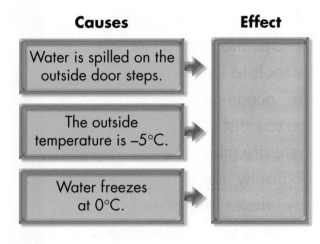

Causes   **Effect**

Water is spilled on the outside door steps.

The outside temperature is −5°C.

Water freezes at 0°C.

 ## Test Prep

Choose the letter that best completes the statement or answers the question.

15. About 75 percent of Earth's surface is covered by

   Ⓐ air.   Ⓑ water.
   Ⓒ plants.   Ⓓ animals.

16. The step in the water cycle in which water forms water vapor in the air is called

   Ⓕ evaporation.
   Ⓖ condensation.
   Ⓗ precipitation.
   Ⓘ groundwater.

17. When the temperature of water falls below 0 degrees Celsius, the water will

   Ⓐ evaporate.
   Ⓑ shrink.
   Ⓒ freeze.
   Ⓓ condense.

18. Wetlands help refill the groundwater supply when

   Ⓕ water evaporates.
   Ⓖ water seeps down into the ground.
   Ⓗ the winds blow.
   Ⓘ water freezes.

19. Explain why the answer you chose for Question 17 is best. For each of the answers you did not choose, give a reason why it is not the best choice.

20.  Writing in Science

Persuasive Practice writing a letter to the editor of your town newspaper. Explain why you think it is important for everyone in your town to conserve water, rather than waste it.

Oceanographer

Oceanographers learn skills to study the ocean using many special tools.

Oceanographers study the water of the ocean, the area beneath it, and the living things in it. Would you like to sail the deep blue sea? Then think about being an oceanographer. Oceanographers are scientists. They use tools to keep track of ocean temperatures, ocean currents, and life in the ocean. These scientists study the ocean as a whole, but there are many specific jobs in the field of oceanography. For example, you might want to study whales and other living things in the ocean. Then you can become a marine biologist. Do you like to tinker with tools and gadgets? Maybe you could be an engineer who designs the special equipment needed to study the underwater world.

Becoming an oceanographer requires four years of college.

Lab zone Take-Home Activity

Choose one specific job you might like to do as an oceanographer. Use resources at home to find out more about the job.

EC CRU 1 0 9 8 7 6 5 4 3 2 1

Chapter 6
Weather

You Will Discover

- patterns of weather.
- how people measure and predict weather.
- ways people stay safe during storms.

online
Student Edition
pearsonsuccessnet.com

How does weather follow patterns?

weather

hurricane

tornado

170

Chapter 6 Vocabulary

weather page 175

atmosphere page 176

hurricane page 182

tornado page 182

blizzard page 183

atmosphere

blizzard

171

Explore How can you measure wind speed?

Materials

Pattern for a Wind Speed Meter

scissors

25 cm piece of string

metric ruler

tape

table-tennis ball

What to Do

1 Make a wind speed meter.

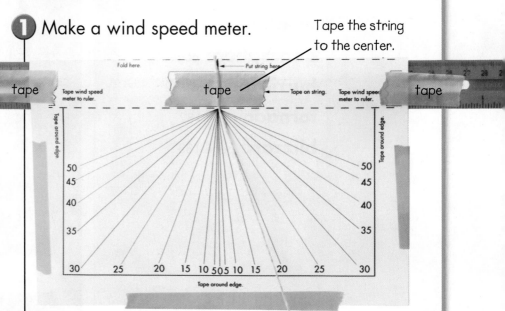

Tape the string to the center.

Fold here. Put string here

tape   Tape wind speed meter to ruler.   tape   Tape on string.   Tape wind speed meter to ruler.   tape

Tape around edge.

50   50
45   45
40   40
35   35

30 25 20 15 10 5 0 5 10 15 20 25 30

Tape around edge.

Tape the string to the ball.

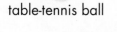

2 Go outside. Point the ruler into the wind. Hold it level with the ground. Read the wind speed.

3 **Measure** and record the wind speed for 1 week. **Observe** at the same time each day. Look for a pattern.

You may also wish to record temperature and air pressure. Check if a thermometer and barometer are available.

Explain Your Results

Infer Suppose you use a heavier ball on the wind gauge. What else would you have to change? Explain.

How to Read Science

TARGET SKILL

Make Inferences

A writer doesn't always tell us everything. As you read, you might have to put some facts together.

When you make an **inference**, you explain an event or a thing.

- You use facts you read.
- You use your own experiences.
- You make a guess from what you observe or from what you already know.

Weather Report

The weather this morning appears sunny and warm. Winds are beginning to blow out of the northwest. The northwest region reported cloudy and cool conditions last evening. Rain began to fall there this morning.

Apply It!

Study this graphic organizer. Make a graphic organizer like this one. List the facts from the weather report in your graphic organizer. Write your inference.

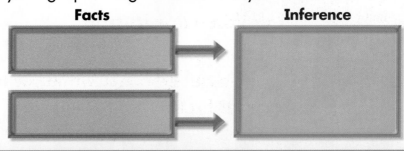

Facts   Inference

You Are There!

You are playing outside on a sunny day. Suddenly you hear a loud rumble in the sky. You look up. Huge black clouds are moving toward you. You see a flash of lightning in the distance. Uh-oh! Here comes a big change in the weather. What caused it? Time to get to safety.

AudioText

What makes up weather?

Weather changes all the time. Measuring weather helps people predict weather accurately.

Parts of Weather

What will the weather be like this weekend? Will it be sunny or rainy? **Weather** is what the air is like outside. It includes the kinds of clouds in the sky and the kind and amount of water in the air. It also includes the temperature of the air and how the wind is blowing.

Clouds are made of water droplets in the air. Different kinds of clouds form in different weather. Because of this, clouds can help predict what will happen to the weather. Some kinds of clouds form in sunny weather. Others form in rainy or stormy weather.

Look at clouds on a warm, bright day. The clouds are white and fluffy. On a stormy day, clouds are dark.

These cumulus clouds look a little like balls of cotton. You see these on sunny days.

These are very high, thin cirrus clouds. They are made of tiny ice crystals. You see these clouds on sunny days too.

1. ✓**Checkpoint** How do clouds look on stormy days?

2. **Writing** in Science   **Narrative** Write a paragraph in your **science journal** that tells what the weather would be like on a perfect day for you. Explain why you like this weather.

175

Parts of the Atmosphere

The space shuttle circles the Earth here.

This is where our atmosphere meets outer space.

Have you ever seen a shooting star? This is where pieces of rock from outer space burn up.

Many jet airplanes fly here above the weather.

Weather happens in the lower part of the atmosphere.

The Atmosphere

The **atmosphere** is the blanket of air that surrounds Earth. This air is made up of gases that have no color, taste, or odor. The temperature is different in different parts of the atmosphere. Weather happens in the lower part of the atmosphere.

The atmosphere has weight, so it presses down on Earth. This pressing down is called air pressure. When the air presses down a lot, the air pressure is high. When it presses less, the air pressure is low.

Describing Weather

You may say the weather is too hot today. Someone else might not agree. That person might like the weather. Words like *hot* mean different things to different people. But 34° Celsius (93° Fahrenheit) means just one thing. It is a fact that describes the temperature of the air. Scientists use special tools to help them describe and measure the weather.

Measuring and Predicting

Scientists can measure air pressure with a tool called a barometer. Scientists use measurements of air pressure to predict changes in weather. Weather reports often describe air pressure. Low air pressure often means that weather will be cloudy or rainy. High air pressure often means skies will be clear.

A tool called an anemometer measures wind speed. A wind vane shows the direction of the wind.

Scientists use hygrometers to measure how much water vapor is in the air. The amount of water vapor in the air is called humidity. The humidity is low when air is dry. The humidity is high when air has more water in it. Rain gauges measure liquid water. They show how much rain has fallen.

Weather tools or instruments help scientists learn more about weather. They also help scientists predict what the weather will be like.

1. ✓**Checkpoint** How do tools help scientists describe the weather?

2. **Make Inferences** High pressure is moving into an area. Use this observation and what you know about air pressure to predict the weather change.

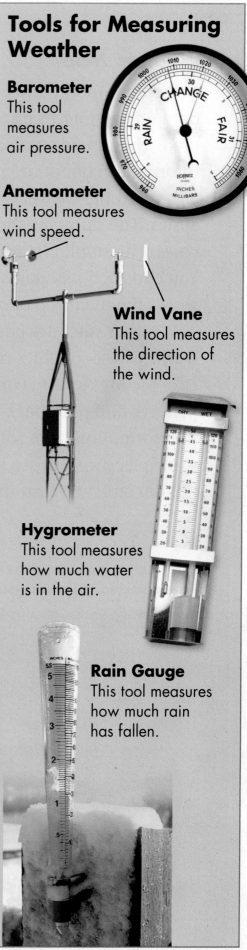

Tools for Measuring Weather

Barometer
This tool measures air pressure.

Anemometer
This tool measures wind speed.

Wind Vane
This tool measures the direction of the wind.

Hygrometer
This tool measures how much water is in the air.

Rain Gauge
This tool measures how much rain has fallen.

Weather Map

Weather tools gather weather data. Scientists show this data on weather maps. Weather maps show data for a large area. They show temperatures and storms. Some maps give information about areas of high and low air pressure.

Look at the weather map below. It shows the United States. The numbers show the temperatures in different cities. The small pictures show what the weather is like. You can probably guess what some pictures mean. The key shows the meaning of all the pictures.

Weather satellites gather weather data from all over the world. These satellites move high above the Earth. They can take pictures of large areas of the planet. They send these pictures and data back to scientists on Earth.

Information from satellites is very useful to scientists. For example, they can see storm clouds form and can tell the direction that the storms are moving.

This weather map uses pictures to interpret data that weather tools have gathered. What can you learn from this weather map?

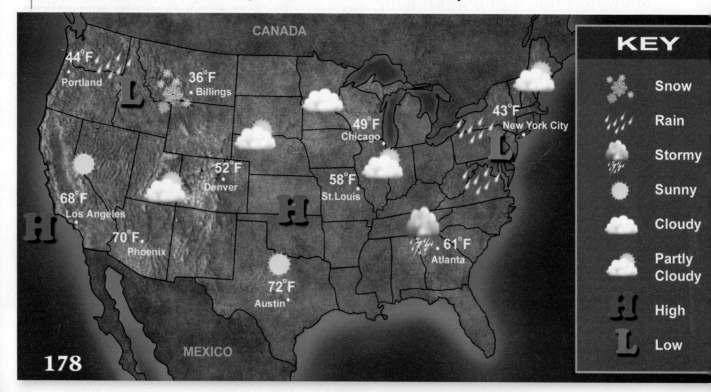

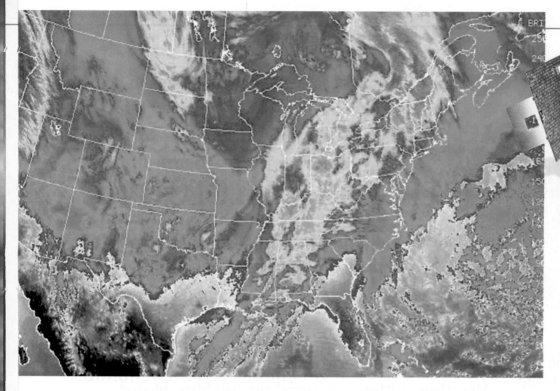

Weather satellites like this one gather weather data.

Maps made from satellite data can show the direction storm clouds are moving.

Pollution Alerts

Weather news may include smog and ozone pollution alerts. In many cities, cars and trucks help cause these alerts. The gases that leave their engines are called exhaust. On some days, a lot of exhaust stays in the air. The Sun's rays can turn that air into smog and ozone. On days with little wind, the smog and ozone do not move away.

Smog and ground-level ozone can be harmful to health. They can make people cough. Some people might not be able to breathe easily. During air pollution alerts, some people must stay inside.

The Sun's rays strike the exhaust from gasoline burned in cars and trucks. This causes smog.

✓ Lesson Checkpoint

1. What can weather maps show?

2. What is one effect that humans can have on weather?

3. **Make Inferences** If there is a smog alert, what can you infer about the weather?

Comparing Temperatures

Places near oceans have different weather patterns than places far from oceans. The tables on page 187 compare the average high and low temperatures in two cities for January and for July. Notice that Seattle is warmer than Indianapolis in January.

July

January

Seattle

Indianapolis

July

January

Tools Take It to the Net
pearsonsuccessnet.com

Average Temperatures in January

	Seattle, Washington	Indianapolis, Indiana
Average High	8°C (46°F)	1°C (34°F)
Average Low	2°C (36°F)	−8°C (18°F)

Average Temperatures in July

	Seattle, Washington	Indianapolis, Indiana
Average High	24°C (75°F)	30°C (86°F)
Average Low	13°C (55°F)	18°C (65°F)

Use the tables and the map to answer the following questions.

1. Use the map to explain why Seattle is usually warmer than Indianapolis in January.

2. What is the average high temperature in July in Seattle? in Indianapolis?

3. What are the average low temperatures in the two cities in July?

4. Which city is usually warmer in July? Use the map to help explain why this is true.

Lab zone Take-Home Activity

Find information about the average high and low temperatures in January and July where you live. Compare these temperatures to the temperatures in Seattle and Indianapolis.

Use Vocabulary

atmosphere (page 176)	**tornado** (page 182)
blizzard (page 183)	**weather** (page 175)
hurricane (page 182)	

Use the vocabulary word from the list above that best completes each sentence.

1. A(n) _____ is a spinning column of air that touches the ground and happens quickly.

2. Temperature, wind speed, and clouds are parts of the _____.

3. A(n) _____ is a huge, strong storm that forms over the warm ocean.

4. A winter storm with low temperatures, strong winds, and lots of blowing snow is a(n) _____.

5. The _____ is made up of gases that surround Earth.

Explain Concepts

6. Why is weather important?

7. If you had tools for measuring parts of the weather, what information could you collect?

8. List some clues that indicate a change in the weather.

9. Give an example of a weather pattern and describe it in detail.

10. How does the National Weather Service help people stay safe?

11. Use the chart below to tell which city has warmer average temperatures in July. Which city has the biggest difference between the average high and average low?

	Birmingham, Alabama	Santa Fe, New Mexico
Average High in July	33°C (91°F)	29°C (85°F)
Average Low in July	21°C (70°F)	12°C (53°F)

Process Skills

12. **Predict** It is a rainy day, but the air pressure is getting higher. How might the weather change?

13. **Infer** How might weather be different if water never evaporated? Explain your answer.

Make Inferences

14. Copy the table below. Fill in the missing inference.

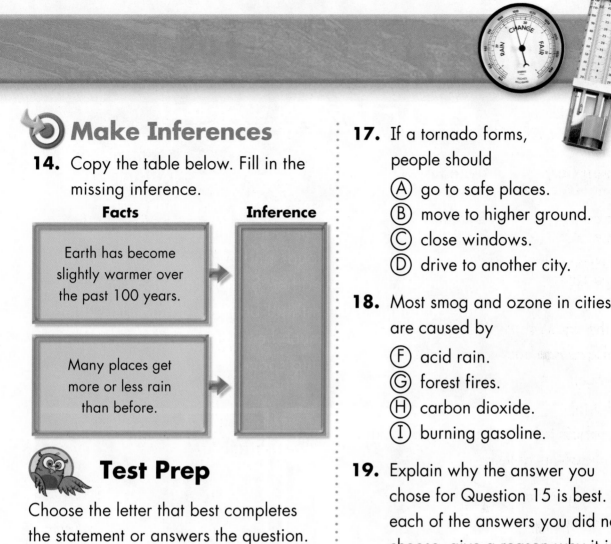

Facts	Inference
Earth has become slightly warmer over the past 100 years.	
Many places get more or less rain than before.	

Test Prep

Choose the letter that best completes the statement or answers the question.

15. What kind of winter weather would a city near the ocean in the western U.S. most likely have?

Ⓐ warm and rainy
Ⓑ warm and snowy
Ⓒ cold and snowy
Ⓓ cool and rainy

16. A severe thunderstorm watch means

Ⓕ a severe thunderstorm is in the area.
Ⓖ a tornado is in the area.
Ⓗ flooding could happen soon.
Ⓘ a thunderstorm might happen.

17. If a tornado forms, people should

Ⓐ go to safe places.
Ⓑ move to higher ground.
Ⓒ close windows.
Ⓓ drive to another city.

18. Most smog and ozone in cities are caused by

Ⓕ acid rain.
Ⓖ forest fires.
Ⓗ carbon dioxide.
Ⓘ burning gasoline.

19. Explain why the answer you chose for Question 15 is best. For each of the answers you did not choose, give a reason why it is not the best choice.

20. Writing in Science
Expository Write a paragraph that describes both helpful and harmful effects that the weather can have on people.

Studying Clouds From
SPACE

You know that NASA studies space. NASA also studies Earth's clouds from space. NASA satellites orbit Earth and use different tools or instruments to collect information about clouds and other parts of the Earth system, including weather. Some of the tools measure the amount of sunlight that bounces off clouds. Other tools measure how much heat is trapped by clouds and how much escapes into space.

Cumulus

Cirrus

Cumulonimbus

Stratus

Clouds are an important part of weather patterns. They are part of the water cycle. They interact with the gases that trap heat and warm Earth. NASA scientists are studying how clouds affect Earth's climate.

Many schools are helping NASA study clouds. Students and teachers at these schools observe and measure clouds and other weather conditions. They are given special times to take their measurements. These are the same times when NASA satellites are recording information for their area.

Cirrostratus

Altocumulus

Lab zone Take-Home Activity

Record your own observations of clouds and the temperature at the time of day you observed them. Collect this data for a week. Organize data into a chart. Decide if the kinds and amounts of clouds affected the temperature.

Air Traffic Controller

You are in the control tower at an airport. You can see all the planes and runways. Computers tell you the height, speed, and course of all aircraft.

As an air traffic controller, you make sure planes take off and land safely. You give pilots directions so they can keep their planes a safe distance from other planes. You also give them information about weather patterns. Pilots need to know about any storms. They also must know about sudden changes in the speed or direction of the wind. They need to know what the weather is like near the airport. Is it foggy, snowing, or rainy? Is it clear? The information you give pilots helps keep them and their passengers safe.

People who become air traffic controllers usually have four years of college. Then they must take tests to make sure they would make good air traffic controllers.

Lab zone Take-Home Activity

Suppose you are watching planes as they approach an airport. Describe the information that you need to give the pilots.

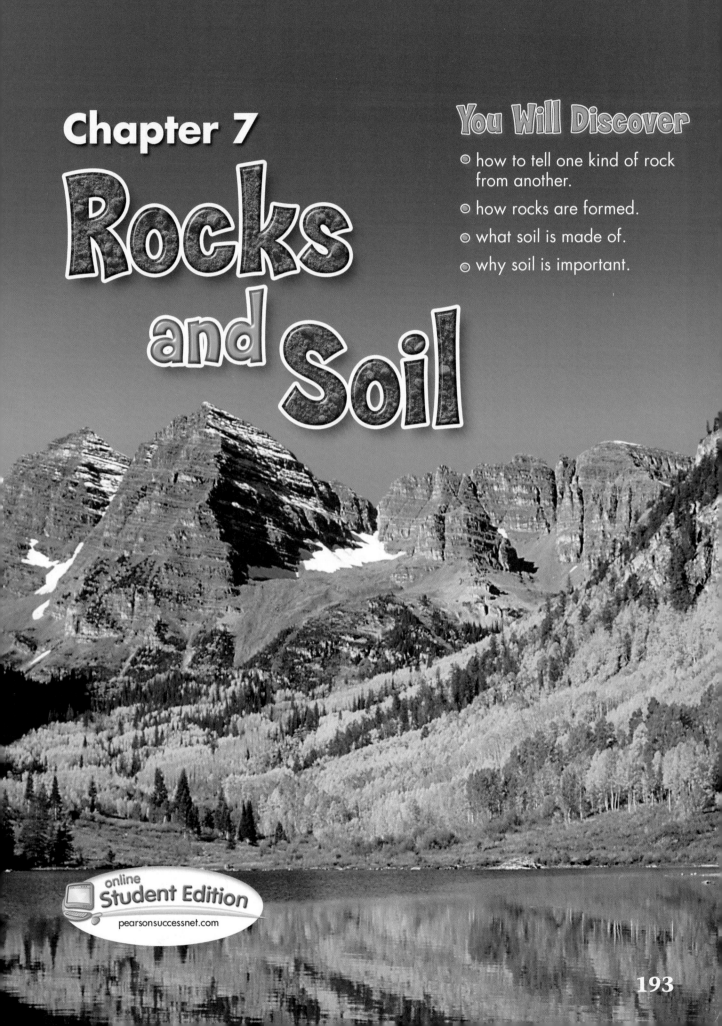

Chapter 7
Rocks and Soil

online
Student Edition
pearsonsuccessnet.com

193

What are some kinds of rocks and soils?

rock

igneous rock

sedimentary rock

metamorphic rock

194

Chapter 7 Vocabulary

rock page 199

mineral page 199

igneous rock page 200

sedimentary rock page 200

metamorphic rock page 201

soil page 206

decay page 206

nutrient page 206

loam page 209

loam

soil

mineral

decay

The slow breaking down of the remains of living things in soil

nutrient

Material in soil that plants need to grow

195

Explore What can you learn from rock layers?

Wind, water, or ice can carry away sand and other materials. Often these materials are dropped in places in layers. Over time, the materials can join together to form rock. This is one reason rocks are often found in layers. In this model the layers of rock are shown by the sand, salt, coffee, sugar, and clay soil.

Materials

small measuring cup and large cup

sand, salt, coffee

sugar and clay soil

small paper clip
rubber band
piece of crayon

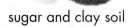

Process Skills

A **model** of something is different from the real thing but can be used to learn something about the real thing.

What to Do

1 **Make a model** of rock layers. Fill the small cup with sand. Pour it into a large cup. Put a paper clip in the sand. Place it touching the side of the cup. The paper clip stands for a fossil animal.

2 Add layers of the other materials to the cup. Place a "fossil animal" (a rubber band or a piece of crayon) in 2 of the layers.

clay soil
crayon
sugar
coffee
rubber band
salt
paper clip
sand

Explain Your Results

1. Which layer was added first? Which layer in your **model** is the "oldest"? How do you know?

2. **Infer** Where would you expect to find an older fossil—in an upper layer of rock or in a lower layer? Explain.

How to Read Science

TARGET SKILL

Compare and Contrast

When you **compare** things, you tell how they are alike. When you **contrast** things, you tell how they are different.

- Words and phrases such as *similar, like, all, both,* or *in the same way* are clues that things are being compared.

- Words and phrases such as *different, unlike,* or *in a different way* are clues that things are being contrasted.

Magazine Article

Rock Collectors

Ben and Misha both collect rocks. Ben prefers brightly colored rocks. He is a member of a rock hunters club that goes on collecting trips. Misha has a different way of collecting his favorite kinds of rocks—fossil rocks. His uncle sends Misha fossil rocks from all around the world. Unlike Ben, Misha just has to make a trip to his mailbox to add to his collection.

Apply It!

You can use a graphic organizer as a **model** to show how things compare and contrast.

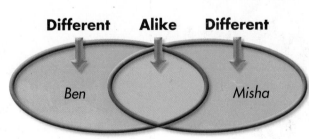

Different   Alike   Different

Ben   Misha

Use a graphic organizer to show ways that Ben and Misha are alike and different in the way they collect rocks.

You Are There!

Be careful as you climb on the rocks. It's a good thing you have on hiking boots. They will help you climb. Can you see that some of the rocks have sharp edges? Some look rough. Others look smooth. There are differences in color. What are rocks made of and where do they come from?

AudioText

How do rocks form?

Rocks are everywhere. Some are as large as a mountain. Others are smaller than a grain of sand. Minerals make up rock. Rock forms in different ways.

Rocks

Earth consists of mostly different kinds of rocks. **Rock** is natural, solid, nonliving material made of one or more minerals. A **mineral** is a natural material that forms from nonliving matter.

You can tell rocks apart by looking at their physical properties. The physical properties of rocks include color, what minerals they are made of, and texture.

The rocks you see here range in color from gray to brown. Sometimes the minerals are so small that they aren't easy to see. Texture is the size of the bits of minerals, or grains, that make up the rock. Some rocks may have grains that are big enough to see. These different sizes of minerals make rocks feel smooth, rough, or bumpy.

1. ✓**Checkpoint** What are some physical properties of rocks?

2. **Compare and Contrast** How are the rocks shown in the pictures alike? How are they different?

Rock Groups

Rocks can be placed into three main groups. Rocks in each group formed in a certain way. Each group contains many kinds of rocks.

Igneous rock forms from a very hot mixture of melted minerals and gases. This mixture may cool slowly below ground until it hardens. Then the mineral grains may be large. If the rock cools quickly above ground or on the ocean floor, the grains may be too small to see.

Another group of rocks form from sediments, which are tiny bits of rock, sand, shells and other materials. Sediments settle to the bottom of rivers, lakes, and oceans. Over thousands of years, the sediments are pressed together and cemented into **sedimentary rock.** Sedimentary rock forms in layers—one layer at a time.

Fossils of extinct plants and animals can be found in sedimentary rocks. Their bodies were buried in sand and mud that hardened into rock. Fossils in sedimentary rock can show the history of life over time.

Fossils in Sedimentary Rock

Crinoids were ancient animals that looked like plants.

Trilobites were like modern crabs.

Ammonites looked similar to today's snails.

Metamorphic rock is rock that has been changed by heat and pressure. Shale is a sedimentary rock. Heat and pressure underground change the minerals in the shale. The shale becomes slate, a metamorphic rock. Granite is an igneous rock. It can be changed into gneiss, a metamorphic rock.

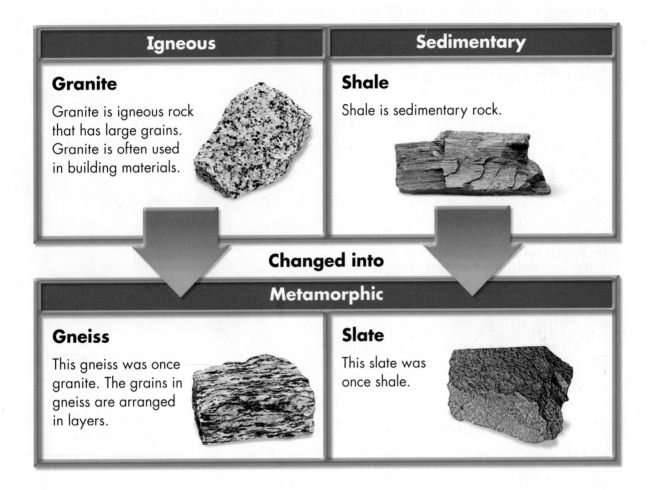

Igneous

Granite

Granite is igneous rock that has large grains. Granite is often used in building materials.

Sedimentary

Shale

Shale is sedimentary rock.

Changed into

Metamorphic

Gneiss

This gneiss was once granite. The grains in gneiss are arranged in layers.

Slate

This slate was once shale.

✓ **Lesson Checkpoint**

1. How is igneous rock that forms above ground different from igneous rock that forms below ground?

2. Describe clues, found in sedimentary rock, which show that living things have changed over time.

3. **Writing** in Science   **Expository** List facts in your **science journal** about the three kinds of rocks. Then write a paragraph describing each of the three kinds.

What are minerals?

Minerals are the most common solid material found on Earth. Gold and silver are rare minerals. Rock salt and quartz are common minerals.

Identifying Minerals

Color is a property you notice easily about a mineral. But some minerals can be found in different colors. For example, the mineral quartz can be pink, purple, yellow, brown, white, or black. Other minerals always have the same color.

A better way to identify a mineral is by the color in its powder form. When you rub a mineral across a rough surface, it may leave a streak mark or powder. The color of these effects are always the same even if two pieces of the mineral are different colors.

Luster is a property that shows how a mineral reflects light. Minerals can be metallic, pearly, silky, greasy, glassy, or dull.

The mineral magnetite has the property of magnetism. Objects that contain iron are pulled to the magnetite.

Vinegar fizzes on limestone that contains the mineral calcite. The fizzing happens because the vinegar reacts with the calcite. The reaction gives off carbon dioxide.

Properties of Minerals

Mineral	Color	Luster	Streak	Hardness
Mica Mica breaks into flaky pieces when struck.	black, gray, green, violet	pearly on surfaces	white	can be scratched with a knife
Molybdenite This mineral is one of the strongest and most commonly used heat-resistant metals.	silvery	metallic	bluish gray	can be scratched with a fingernail
Crocoite Much of this mineral comes from Australia.	reddish-orange	very shiny	orange-yellow	can be scratched with a coin

Another way to identify a mineral is to test its hardness. Some minerals, such as talc, are so soft you can scratch them with your fingernail. The hardest mineral is diamond. It can be scratched only by another diamond.

Some minerals can be identified by their appearance. Gold, for example, appears sometimes in nugget form. Other minerals can be identified by taste, smell, or touch.

1. ✅ **Checkpoint** What are ways to identify minerals?

2. 🎯 **Compare and Contrast** How are rocks and minerals alike? How are they different? Use a graphic organizer to show your answer.

How the Body Uses Minerals

These are some ways that the body uses minerals.

Mineral	How Used
Calcium	Helps form bones and teeth and helps cause muscles to contract
Chromium	Helps change digested food into energy
Copper	Helps form skin and other tissues
Iron	Carries oxygen in blood to all parts of the body
Potassium	Helps nerves and muscles work
Phosphorus	Helps release energy and form bones and teeth
Sodium	Helps control water levels and carry messages through nerves

How We Use Minerals

It is almost impossible to go through a day without using minerals. The cavity-fighting fluoride in your toothpaste came from the mineral fluorite. The glass you look through in your window came from the minerals quartz, soda ash, and limestone. The salt in your food is the mineral halite. The metal in your spoon is a mineral. Even the graphite that you write with in your pencil is a mineral. Almost everything we use is made from minerals or contains minerals.

Minerals Keep Us Healthy

People also need minerals to keep their bodies healthy and full of energy. Many of these minerals are found in plants. Green leafy vegetables, such as spinach, contain calcium. Iron is found in fruit and green vegetables. Sodium in vegetables such as celery, and potassium in fruits work together to help transmit nerve impulses and control muscles. Almost everything we eat has some minerals in it.

✓ Lesson Checkpoint

1. What is a mineral?
2. Why are minerals important to your health?
3. **Writing in Science** **Expository** In your **science journal** list five things you did today that used minerals. Use a chart with two columns. Head the first column, *Activity*. Head the second, *Mineral*.

Other Ways We Use Minerals

Halite

The mineral halite is crushed and then ground up. We use it to flavor and preserve food. (We know this mineral as table salt.)

Copper

The mineral copper is found in igneous rock. The rocks are mined from the ground. When the rocks are crushed and heated, the copper becomes separated from the rock. Then, the copper can be made into objects such as pots and pans.

Fluorite

The mineral fluorite is found in many rocks, such as granite. The rocks are crushed and the fluorite is separated out. Then, it is used to make many products such as toothpaste.

Lead

Lead is found in a mineral known as galena. The rocks are crushed and heated to produce lead. Lead is put into aprons such as the ones shown to protect people while X-ray pictures are taken.

Iron

Iron is a mineral found in the rock called hematite. The rocks are crushed and heated. Then, iron in the melted material is separated out. Iron is mixed with other materials to make steel. Steel is used for many tools and machines.

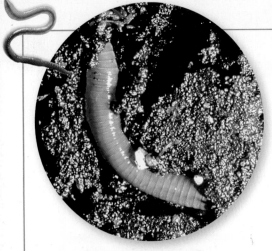
Earthworms mix up the topsoil as they dig through it. That improves the soil.

We depend on topsoil to grow our food.

Soil must pack down hard and stay firm so that houses built on it don't shift.

Why is soil important?

Soil is an important part of the system that supports all life on land. Soil and parts of soil have different properties.

Parts of Soil

Soil is the thin layer of loose material that covers most of Earth's land. Soil is not simply dirt. Natural processes develop soil over a long period of time. It takes hundreds of years for nature to rebuild lost topsoil. Soil has the material plants need to grow.

Squeeze a handful of soil and see that it's more than bits of rock. Soil might clump together because it holds water and material that was once living.

Living things in soil break down the remains of plants and animals. This process is called **decay.** Decay releases things plants need in order to grow. Each of these things is a **nutrient.** Some minerals also release nutrients. Water and nutrients support most plants on land, including crops. When you think about it, soil is more valuable than gold!

Soil Layers

Soil is organized into layers. Different places have layers of different thicknesses and color.

Topsoil

Topsoil is the top layer. Topsoil includes rock particles mixed with the dark products of decay. The decayed parts of plant and animal remains are called humus. Humus contains much of what plants need to grow.

Subsoil

Subsoil is under topsoil. It is often lighter in color than topsoil. It doesn't have as much humus as topsoil. Subsoil includes pieces of broken rocks. Tree roots grow into the subsoil. Water from precipitation may be in this layer.

Bedrock

As this rock breaks down, it provides raw material for making new soil.

1. **Checkpoint** What is soil made of?

2. **Math in Science** Suppose it takes 1,500 years for 1 centimeter of soil to form in a certain place. How long would it take for 2 centimeters of soil to form? Show your work.

207

Comparing Soils

Soil is not the same everywhere. Soil near your home may be different than soil at your school. The kind of soil depends in part on the types of rock particles that help make up the soil. Sand, silt, and clay are the three main types of particles found in soil. They differ in size. Sand particles are the largest. Clay particles are the smallest.

Sand

Large spaces in sand allow water to easily pass through. Roots of many plants in sandy soil may not have time to soak up the water. Sandy soil feels rough and gritty.

Silt

The medium-sized particles in silt are more closely packed together. Although water passes through silt, silty soil also holds water well.

About Loam

Loam is good soil for growing plants. The graph shows the amount of each ingredient in loam.

- Sand, Silt, Clay
- Air
- Water
- Humus

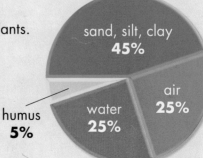

sand, silt, clay
45%

air
25%

water
25%

humus
5%

208

All soil has the same four ingredients. Weathered rocks containing minerals make up most of the soil. Humus makes up another part. Humus is made up of decaying plants and animals. Humus is a very important part of soil. Air and water fill in the spaces between particles of rock and humus.

Most soils are a mixture of sand, silt, and clay. Soils with this mixture are called **loam.** Loam also contains humus, which has many minerals and other nutrients. Loam soil with its minerals, humus, air, and water is a very good mixture for growing most plants. Loam soils hold onto water loosely enough for plant roots to soak it up.

Clay
Clay particles are the smallest. Water passes slowly into clay. Once clay absorbs water, the particles hold tightly together. Very wet clay feels smooth and sticky.

√ Lesson Checkpoint

1. Explain the importance of soil.

2. Compare the ability of sand, silt, and clay to hold water.

3. **Social Studies** in Science Find information about states that have many large farms. Find out which fruits, vegetables, and grains grow in each area.

Investigate How much water can soil hold?

Materials

small measuring cup

3 clear plastic cups and
3 foam cups

sandy, clay, and loam soils

hand lens and pencil

paper towel and scissors

spoon and masking tape

graduated cylinder
(or measuring cup)

water

Process Skills

By **measuring** carefully, you can find out which type of soil can hold the most water.

What to Do

① Get 60 mL of each type of soil.

Label the cups.

sandy soil
clay soil
loam soil

② **Observe** the soil samples with a hand lens. Describe their properties (color, texture).

sandy soil
loam soil
clay soil

③ Punch 10 holes in the bottom of each foam cup.

④ Set each cup on the paper towel and trace around the bottom. Cut out the 3 circles you traced and put one inside each cup, over the holes.

5 Put each of your soil samples into a different foam cup. Pack down the soil using a spoon.

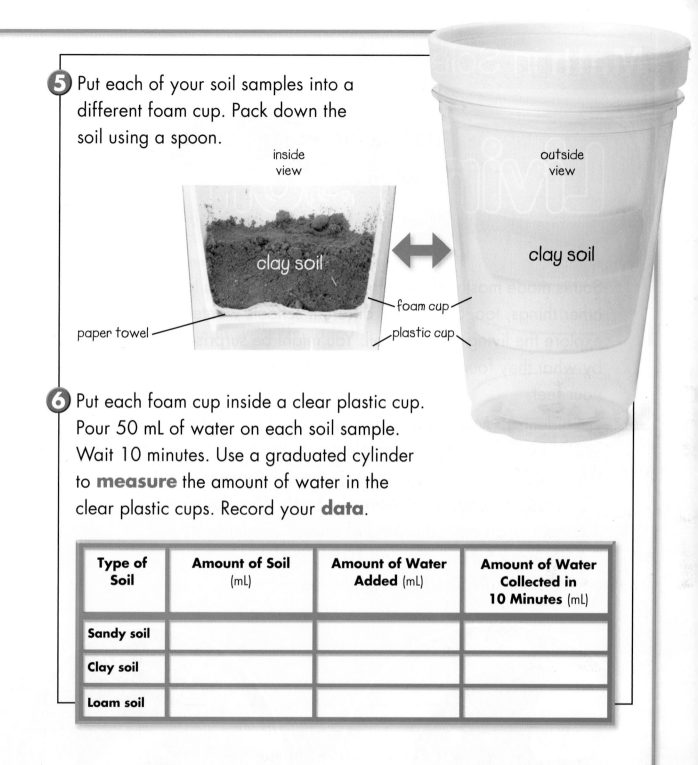

inside view

outside view

clay soil

clay soil

paper towel

foam cup

plastic cup

6 Put each foam cup inside a clear plastic cup. Pour 50 mL of water on each soil sample. Wait 10 minutes. Use a graduated cylinder to **measure** the amount of water in the clear plastic cups. Record your **data**.

Type of Soil	Amount of Soil (mL)	Amount of Water Added (mL)	Amount of Water Collected in 10 Minutes (mL)
Sandy soil			
Clay soil			
Loam soil			

Explain Your Results

1. Describe the color, texture, and other properties of each soil you **observed**. What do you think each is made of?

2. Based on your **measurements**, which type of soil holds the most water? the least?

Go Further

In which soil would desert plants grow best? Make a plan to answer this or another question you may have.

Chapter 7 Review and Test Prep

Use Vocabulary

decay
(page 206)

mineral
(page 199)

igneous rock
(page 200)

nutrient
(page 206)

loam
(page 209)

rock (page 199)

metamorphic
rock (page 201)

sedimentary
rock (page 200)

soil (page 206)

Use the vocabulary word from the list above that best completes each sentence.

1. Rock made up of layers of sediment that have hardened is _____.

2. Most of the land is covered with a thin layer of loose material called _____.

3. A(n) _____ is a natural material that makes up rock.

4. When living things _____, they break down, or rot.

5. Soil that is a mixture of sand, silt, clay, minerals, and decayed matter is called _____.

6. Any kind of solid, nonliving material found on Earth and made of minerals is a(n) _____.

7. Each type of small particle that plants take into their roots is a(n) _____, found in good growing soil.

8. Rock that has changed to another type of rock by heat and pressure is _____.

9. Rock that forms when melted Earth materials cool and harden is _____.

Explain Concepts

10. What is one way that sedimentary rock forms?

11. Explain why a bone is not considered a mineral.

12. Describe the layers of soil from top to bottom.

13. Predict Which would dry faster after it rains: a sandy beach or a grassy field? Give a reason for your answer.

14. Model Make a model or a drawing that shows the different layers of soil.

15. Infer You observe that a mineral sample can be scratched with a coin. What do you infer about the hardness of the mineral?

Compare and Contrast

16. Make a graphic organizer like the one below. Fill it in to compare and contrast sandy soil and clay soil.

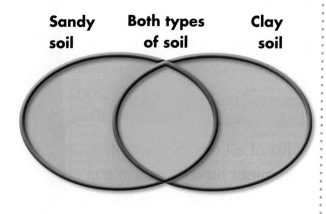

| Sandy soil | Both types of soil | Clay soil |

Test Prep

Choose the letter that best completes the statement or answers the question.

17. All rocks contain
  - (A) loam.
  - (B) minerals.
  - (C) water.
  - (D) sediments.

18. In what rocks are fossils most often found?
  - (F) sedimentary
  - (G) igneous
  - (H) metamorphic
  - (I) all of the above

19. The layer of soil just below the topsoil is
  - (A) loam.
  - (B) decayed matter.
  - (C) rock.
  - (D) subsoil.

20. Writing in Science
Persuasive Write a letter to a member of a city council that discusses why rich farmland is valuable to everyone in the community.

Dr. Elissa R. Levine

Dr. Levine's interest in soil began when she was a child.

Dr. Levine is a Soil Scientist for NASA's Goddard Space Flight Center. She has been interested in soil for a long time. She once said, "When I was little my mother sat me in the soil and showed me all kinds of interesting things to look at and play with. I've been interested in the soil ever since."

Dr. Levine gathers information from pictures taken by satellites that travel high over Earth. The pictures tell about our environment. She also studies the ways that soil changes all around the world. She is trying to find the causes of these changes.

Dr. Levine also teaches about soil to students all over the world. The students gather data about soil. Dr. Levine uses the information to make computer models of the soils. She has found that soil connects all the other parts of our environment together.

Lab zone Take-Home Activity

Make a list of all the things that Dr. Levine might have found in soil when she was a child. How would each thing help the soil?

EC CRU 10 9 8 7 6 5 4 3 2 1

You Will Discover

- layers of the Earth
- how some forces change Earth's surface quickly.
- how other forces change Earth's surface slowly.

Chapter 8

Changes on Earth

online
Student Edition
pearsonsuccessnet.com

Discovery Channel School
Student DVD
DISCOVERY CHANNEL SCHOOL

How do forces cause changes on Earth's surface?

magma

lava

landform

218

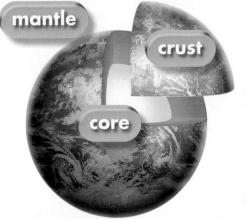

mantle

crust

core

Chapter 8 Vocabulary

crust page 223

mantle page 223

core page 223

landform page 224

magma page 226

lava page 226

weathering page 230

erosion page 232

weathering

erosion

219

Explore How do some mountains form?

Materials

clay

waxed paper

What to Do

1 Make a **model** of one way mountains can form. First, make flat layers of clay. Then, stack the layers on waxed paper.

2 Next, push on the ends of the clay. Keep the clay on the waxed paper.

surface of the Earth

Push!

Push!

layers of rock

In real life this change would be too slow to see.

Do not change what you record just because your results are different from those of someone else.

3 Finally, record what happens to your model. Make a sketch or diagram.

Explain Your Results

1. This model shows a way some mountains form. Think about the layers of rock in this type of mountain. Do you think the layers will be mostly tilted or mostly level? Explain.

2. Compare and contrast your model and a real mountain. How does **using the model** help you learn about real mountains?

Process Skills

When scientists **use a model** to help learn about a real thing, they compare and contrast the model and the real thing.

How to Read Science

Sequence

A **sequence** is a series of actions that take place in a certain order.

- A writer might use clue words such as *first, then, next,* and *finally* to show a sequence.
- An artist might use numbers and labels in a drawing to show a sequence.

Science Article

Eruption

How does a volcano erupt? First, pressure and heat melt rock within the Earth. This material is magma, a hot, thick liquid mixed with gases. Then, some of the material rises through cracks in the rock above it. Next, the liquid rock and gases build up pressure on the rock at the surface. Finally, the pressure gets so great that liquid rock, gases, and bits of rock come out of the ground.

Apply It!

Make a sequence to **model** how a volcano forms. Place information you read into a graphic organizer like this one.

First
↓
Then
↓
Next
↓
Finally

What is that billowing cloud on the horizon? What is making that rumbling sound? Is there a storm forming over there? No, it's a volcano erupting! The cloud above the volcano rises miles high. The Sun disappears behind the huge plume of smoke and ash. What force could cause such a tremendous change?

What are Earth's layers?

Mantle

Crust

Core

If you could remove a big chunk of Earth, you would see that it is made up of layers.

Earth's Layers

Earth can be divided into three main layers. You live on the outer layer of Earth—the **crust.** Earth's crust is made of different kinds of rock. The thickness of the crust varies from place to place. Its thickness under the continents is about 37 kilometers (23 miles). That may seem pretty thick. If you compare all the Earth to a peach, however, the Earth's crust would be just the skin.

Beneath the crust lies the **mantle.** Earth's mantle is made of very hot igneous and metamorphic rock. It may flow like oozing toothpaste.

The **core** is the innermost layer of Earth. It is made of metal. The core is hot enough to melt. The center of the core is packed together so tightly, however, that it remains mostly solid. The much larger outer part of the core is a very hot, dense liquid.

1. ✓**Checkpoint** What is Earth's core like?

2. **Writing** in Science **Expository** Compare Earth's layers to the parts of a peach. Make a labeled drawing in your **science journal**. Then, write a paragraph that compares the two.

Shapes on Earth's Surface

Does the land near you have mountains, hills, and valleys? Each is an example of a **landform.** Landforms are the solid features formed on Earth's crust. Other features include bodies of water.

Many forces shape landforms. These forces come from above and below Earth's crust. Moving water, though, is the main force. For example, rivers can act like saws. Pebbles and sand in the moving water slowly cut through rock. Flooding rivers deposit pebbles, sand, and silt on their banks. These processes help shape valleys. Notice how many of the landforms below were shaped by water.

Glacier
A glacier is a large, moving body of ice. It forms in cold places where snow and ice pile up year after year. It slowly moves downhill.

Valley
A valley is a low, narrow area on the crust. Some valleys are formed by rivers, while others are formed by glaciers.

Plateau
A plateau is a plain that is higher than the land around it.

Ocean
The ocean is the salt water that covers almost three-fourths of Earth's surface.

Coast
The coast is land next to the ocean, which helps to shape the coastline.

Volcano

A volcano is an opening in Earth's crust through which hot, melted rock is forced up by pressure inside the Earth.

Mountain

A mountain is a landform high above the land around it. Some mountains form when blocks of rock are pushed up or drop down along cracks in the Earth's crust.

River

A river is a natural stream of water that helps to shape the valley or plain it passes through.

Hill

A hill is a high place on the Earth's surface, but not as high as a mountain. Hills often have rounded tops.

Plain

A plain is a large, mostly flat area.

Lake

A lake forms when the flow of water slows enough to fill an area.

✓ Lesson Checkpoint

1. Contrast Earth's crust, mantle, and core.

2. **Sequence** List the events that occur as rivers move through rock.

3. **Art in Science** Draw a picture that has mountains and valleys. Write how they might have formed on your picture.

225

What are volcanoes and earthquakes?

Volcanoes and earthquakes cause rapid and sometimes dangerous changes in the landscape.

How Do Volcanoes Form?

Volcanoes begin deep within the mantle where **magma** forms. Magma is hot, pasty rock that moves within the mantle. Magma close to the suface melts and flows easily because the pressure is less. Magma can gush out of weak spots in the crust, aided by the pressure of gases it contains. A volcano is an opening out of which this hot material erupts.

An eruption is like opening a can of shaken soda. Bubbles of gas separate from the liquid and force the liquid out. Material that erupts from a volcano contains ash, cinders, and hot, molten rock called **lava.** As lava cools and hardens, it becomes igneous rock. That's brand-new crust! If the rock builds to great heights, a mountain or island forms.

Volcanoes

Magma collects in large pockets called magma chambers. As magma leaves the chamber, it moves up a tunnel or central vent. Sometimes, magma escapes from the central vent and erupts from side vents. Most magma, however, erupts at the top of the volcano through a bowl-shaped crater.

The red hot lava from this volcano hisses as it meets the cool water.

This volcano in Hawaii lacks a billowing cloud of ash because the erupting material contains little gas.

Some volcanoes grow into mountains as igneous rock from many eruptions builds up around the opening in the crust.

Crater

Central vent

3 When magma erupts from the volcano, it is called lava.

4 The lava cools and hardens, forming igneous rock. The rock builds up. If it builds up high enough, it forms a mountain.

2 Magma pushes upward through cracks and weak spots in Earth's crust.

Magma chamber

1 Magma forms deep within Earth's mantle. It gathers underground in magma chambers.

1. ✓**Checkpoint** What does lava become when it cools?

2. **Social Studies** in Science Look at a world map. Find one volcano on each of Earth's continents. Make a table to organize your information.

227

Earthquakes

Have you ever built a play house out of flimsy cardboard? A sudden bump sends vibrations through the house and it can fall over. In a similar way, sudden shifts between parts of Earth's crust cause the ground to vibrate in all directions. This shaking is an earthquake. Most earthquakes happen along faults. A fault is a large crack in the Earth's crust.

The vibrations of an earthquake move as waves through the Earth. Waves move back and forth and up and down along Earth's surface. These waves can cause cracks in the Earth's surface. Rubble can pile up in areas where the crust moved.

The 15-second Loma Prieta earthquake in 1989 destroyed this road in Oakland, California.

Earthquake Damage

The damage an earthquake causes depends on how close the earthquake is to the surface and how long the crust shakes. Also, the closer an earthquake is to a city or town, the more damage it can cause to buildings, bridges, and underground pipes.

An earthquake can cause landslides. Landslides are just what you might think they are. They are downhill movements of rocks and earth. The loose surface of the land slides down a slope.

Landslides can happen on the ocean floor or on land. Undersea landslides can form giant waves. Landslides on hills and mountains can ruin homes and destroy roads. They can bury large areas.

Vibrations from an earthquake cause cracks such as this one.

Parts of this parking garage snapped during a 1994 earthquake.

Loose soil and rock slid down this hillside during a landslide.

✓ Lesson Checkpoint

1. Compare and contrast magma and lava.

2. Where do most earthquakes happen? Why?

3. **Sequence** Use a graphic organizer to show the steps in the eruption of a volcano.

229

The growing roots of this tree in Arizona are helping to break the rock apart.

What are weathering and erosion?

Weathering and erosion are forces that change the surface of the Earth.

Weathering

Landforms change constantly. For this to happen, rocks in landforms must first break apart. **Weathering** is any action that breaks rocks into smaller pieces.

Weathering changes can be very slow. Some may take less than a year. Others might take centuries. Weathering goes on all the time.

Plants sometimes cause weathering. Their roots can grow into cracks in rocks. As the roots grow, they can split and break up the rocks.

Water can soak through soil. The water changes the minerals in rock below the soil. The rock is weakened and it begins to break apart.

While in a glacier, this rock became smaller and smoother as forces acted upon it.

Sizes of Rocks

Weathering breaks rocks into smaller and smaller pieces. Water wears many rocks to a smooth and rounded shape. The following lists the order of size from largest to smallest.

Boulder 300 mm

Cobble 100 mm

Pebble 30 mm

Sand 1 mm

Silt Each is a tiny speck!

Clay You need a microscope to see clay particles!

When water freezes and thaws, it can cause weathering. Water can get into cracks in rocks. When water freezes, it expands, or grows larger. The ice pushes against the sides of the cracks. Over the years, the rocks may break apart.

Ice weathers rocks in another way. A glacier is a huge amount of ice that moves slowly over Earth's crust. As a glacier moves, it carries rocks with it. The rocks and ice scrape against the ground. The huge force of this action grinds valleys wide and smooth. When a glacier melts, weathered rocks of all sizes are left on the ground.

1. ✔**Checkpoint** Describe weathering, giving three examples.

2. **Math** in Science Look at the pictures of rocks on this page. How much bigger is a boulder than a cobble? How much smaller is a sand grain than a pebble? How many sand grains could you line up along a meter stick?

It took millions of years for waves carrying sand and pebbles to carve a hole in this cliff.

This island formed as sand settled from moving water. Waves will continue to shape it.

The whole side of this hill has moved down.

Erosion

Sometimes weathered material stays in place. Sometimes it is picked up and slowly or quickly carried to other places. The movement of weathered material is **erosion.** Water, wind, gravity, and glaciers can cause erosion.

Erosion by Water and Wind

Water causes erosion in many places. Rainwater can carry away soil from farm fields. Waves cause erosion along shorelines. Rivers carry bits of rock from place to place. Sand and mud flow over a river's banks during a flood.

New islands can form as a result of erosion. This happens when rivers carry rock and bits of soil to the ocean. These particles build up over time. Some form islands just off the coast. Wind and waves continue to shape these islands.

Erosion by wind is common in dry regions, such as deserts. Wind can carry dry sand and soil to other places. Few tall plants grow in deserts, so there is little to stop the particles from blowing around. The particles bump into rocks and break off tiny grains. Over time, more grains are broken off. The rocks slowly change.

Erosion by Gravity and Living Things

Gravity can cause erosion. Gravity pulls rocks and soil downhill. This material moves slowly on gentle slopes. Weathered material can move quickly on steep slopes. A mudflow is the quick movement of very wet soil. A rockslide is the quick movement of rocks down a slope.

Living things can cause erosion. Ground squirrels tunnel through soil. Worms mix and move soil. Ants move soil to make underground nests. Erosion continues as water and air move through the tunnels.

Map Fact
Water erosion shaped these rocks in Bryce Canyon in Utah. The shapes that look like creatures are called "hoodoos."

Rain and melting snow carved out these rock columns.

✓Lesson Checkpoint

1. How are weathering and erosion different? How are they alike?

2. How does most erosion happen in dry regions?

3. **Writing** in Science   **Expository**
   Use the photos on page 232 and this page to explain in your **science journal** how water is causing erosion.

233

Lab zone Guided Inquiry

Investigate How can you observe erosion?

Materials

safety goggles

small paper cups and pencil

tub and spoon

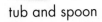

sand, mud, rocks

eraser and ruler

water

Process Skills

Recording your careful **observations** in a chart is one way of **collecting data**.

What to Do

1 Poke 4 holes in the bottom of a paper cup. This is your Rain Cup.

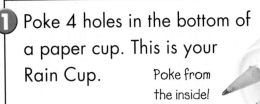

Poke from the inside!

 Wear safety goggles!

2 Put the sand, mud, and rocks into the tub. Blow *gently* on the sand pile, mud pile, and rock pile. **Observe**.

3 Use an eraser to prop up the back edge of the tub. Fill a small paper cup $\frac{1}{2}$ full with water. Hold the Rain Cup 4 cm above the sand. Quickly pour water into the Rain Cup. Observe. **Collect data**. Record your observations in a chart.

	Amount of Erosion by Wind and Water	
	Effect of Blowing	**Effect of Moving Water**
Sand		
Mud		
Rocks		

More Lab zone Activities Take It to the Net
pearsonsuccessnet.com

4 Repeat step 3 for the mud pile and the rock pile.

The eraser props up the back edge and makes the tub tilt forward.

Rain Cup

4 cm

sand pile
3 spoonfuls

mud pile
3 spoonfuls

rock pile
5 rocks

Explain Your Results

1. **Interpret Data** Which caused more erosion, blowing air or moving water? Which was eroded the most, the sand pile, the mud pile, or the rock pile? Which was eroded the least?

2. How is your **model** like what happens in the real world? How is it different? How can your model be used to learn about erosion?

Go Further

How could you change your model to prevent water or wind erosion? Think of a way to solve the problem. Then use your model to test your solution.

Measuring an Earthquake

"The earthquake measured 6.7 on the Richter scale." Did you ever hear a news reporter talk about an earthquake this way? The number tells how strong the earthquake was. The strength of an earthquake depends on how much the rocks along the fault moved and how long the earthquake lasts.

In the table below, 9 earthquakes are listed in order of their strength, from least to greatest.

Some Major California Earthquakes			
Location	Strength	Length of Fault (kilometers)	Time (seconds)
Whittier Narrows	5.9	6	3
North Palm Springs	5.9	20	4
Borrego Mountain	6.5	25	6
Northridge	6.7	14	7
Loma Prieta	7.0	40	15
Landers	7.3	70	24
Kern County	7.5	75	27
San Francisco	7.7	400	110
Fort Tejon	7.8	360	130

WRONG WAY
STOP

Use the table on page 236 to answer these questions.

1. Which earthquake was the strongest?
   A. San Francisco
   B. Kern County
   C. Loma Prieta
   D. Fort Tejon

2. Which earthquake lasted the least amount of time?
   F. Whittier Narrows
   G. Fort Tejon
   H. Landers
   I. Northridge

3. Which earthquake happened along the longest fault?
   A. North Palm Springs
   B. Borrego Mountain
   C. Fort Tejon
   D. San Francisco

4. Which of these statements is true?
   F. Shorter faults produce stronger earthquakes.
   G. Longer faults produce weaker quakes.
   H. Stronger quakes last longer than weaker quakes.
   I. Weaker quakes last longer than stronger quakes.

Lab zone Take-Home Activity

Use the library to find data about these earthquakes: Chile, 1960; Alaska, 1964; Kuril Islands, 1963; Indonesia,1938; and Kamchatka, 1952. Arrange the earthquakes in a table like the one shown. How do these quakes compare with those that struck California?

Chapter 8 Review and Test Prep

Use Vocabulary

core (page 223)	**lava** (page 226)
crust (page 223)	**magma** (page 226)
erosion (page 232)	
	mantle (page 223)
landform (page 224)	**weathering** (page 230)

Use the vocabulary word from the box above that best completes each sentence.

1. Hot, molten rock on Earth's surface is _____.

2. Earth's _____ is the innermost layer of the planet.

3. A hill, a mountain, and a valley are each a(n) _____.

4. The thinnest layer of Earth is the _____.

5. Hot, molten rock that forms deep underground is _____.

6. Magma forms in Earth's thickest layer, which is called the _____.

7. The breaking of rocks into smaller pieces is _____.

8. The moving of weathered materials is _____.

Explain Concepts

9. Which is a better model of Earth's layers, a raw egg or a hard-boiled egg? Explain your choice.

10. Explain how weathering and erosion change Earth's landforms.

11. How do volcanoes change Earth's surface?

12. Compare and contrast erosion that wind causes and erosion that water causes.

Process Skills

13. **Classify** Classify each of the following as either weathering or erosion.
    - (A) a river carrying silt flooding its banks
    - (B) water freezing in the crack of a cliff
    - (C) mud sliding down a hill

14. **Model** Make a series of four drawings to show how a volcano builds up over time.

MindPoint Quiz Show

15. Infer A fault lies between a town with a few buildings and a city with many skyscrapers. The town is 10 miles from the fault. The city is 5 miles from the fault. Infer which area might have the most damage in an earthquake.

Sequence

16. Make a graphic organizer like the one below. Fill in the spaces to show the steps that water may take to weather rocks.

First

Next

Then

Finally

 Test Prep

Choose the letter that best completes the statement or answers the question.

17. Why is Earth's core solid when it is hot enough to melt?

Ⓐ It is in the middle of the planet.

Ⓑ It is smaller than the mantle.

Ⓒ It is made of igneous rocks.

Ⓓ It is under great pressure.

18. What makes water a powerful cause of weathering?

Ⓕ It is a liquid.

Ⓖ It takes up more space when it freezes.

Ⓗ It evaporates.

Ⓘ It rains all the time.

19. Why is erosion by wind so effective in deserts?

Ⓐ Deserts are very moist.

Ⓑ Deserts are very dry.

Ⓒ Deserts are landforms.

Ⓓ Deserts do not have living things.

20. Writing in Science

Narrative Think of being in San Francisco in 1906. That year, a violent earthquake shook the city. Write a paragraph about your experience in this earthquake. Tell what happened during the earthquake and in the week following it.

Dr. Jean Dickey

Dr. Jean Dickey uses views of Earth from space to measure Earth's movements.

As a child growing up in Pennsylvania, Jean Dickey, like her mother, had a strong interest in math and science. While she was still in college, she worked at the Argonne National Laboratory. This laboratory does work in many areas of math and science.

Today, Dr. Dickey is a physicist at NASA's Jet Propulsion Laboratory. One of Dr. Dickey's recent projects was to investigate why Earth appears to be bulging around its middle. That's right! Earth is getting about 1 millimeter "fatter" near the equator each year. After much study, Dr. Dickey and others found two causes for Earth's "weight gain." One is the rapid melting of glaciers. Another is a change in the size and shape of Earth's oceans.

Dr. Dickey's group is also responsible for keeping an eye on Earth's movements in space. They measure and record even the smallest shifts in Earth's place in space. This information is used to help navigate spacecraft.

Lab zone Take-Home Activity

Draw and color a cartoon that shows what is happening to Earth around the equator. Include sentences that explain why it is getting larger.

Chapter 9
Natural Resources

You Will Discover

- ways we use natural resources.
- the difference between renewable and nonrenewable resources.
- ways you can help conserve natural resources.

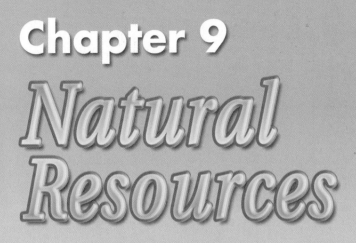

online
Student Edition
pearsonsuccessnet.com

How can people use natural resources responsibly?

natural resource

renewable resource

nonrenewable resource

Chapter 9 Vocabulary

. . . .

natural resource page 247

renewable resource page 247

nonrenewable resource page 248

conservation page 250

recycle page 254

conservation

recycle

Explore How can you classify resources?

A resource is something people use. All the materials on this page come from or are made from resources.

Materials

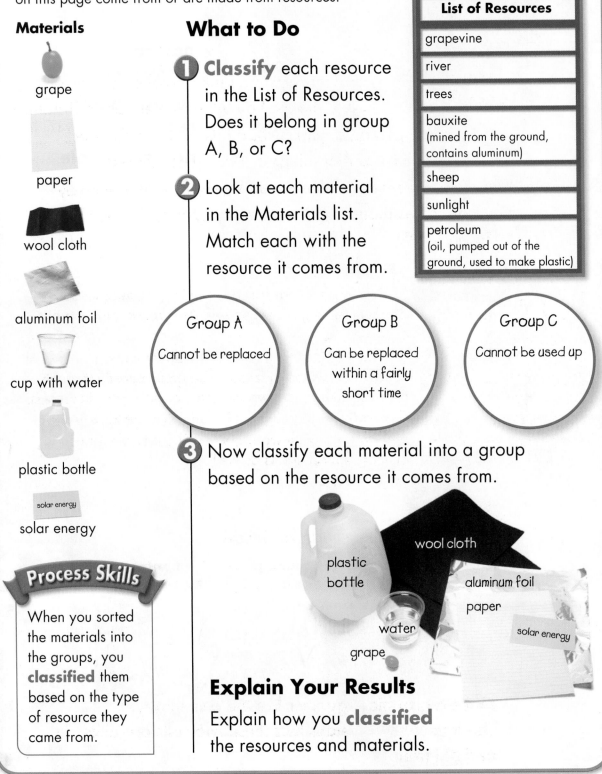

grape

paper

wool cloth

aluminum foil

cup with water

plastic bottle

solar energy

solar energy

What to Do

1 **Classify** each resource in the List of Resources. Does it belong in group A, B, or C?

2 Look at each material in the Materials list. Match each with the resource it comes from.

List of Resources
grapevine
river
trees
bauxite (mined from the ground, contains aluminum)
sheep
sunlight
petroleum (oil, pumped out of the ground, used to make plastic)

Group A
Cannot be replaced

Group B
Can be replaced within a fairly short time

Group C
Cannot be used up

3 Now classify each material into a group based on the resource it comes from.

plastic bottle

wool cloth

aluminum foil

paper

solar energy

water

grape

Explain Your Results

Explain how you **classified** the resources and materials.

Process Skills

When you sorted the materials into the groups, you **classified** them based on the type of resource they came from.

How to Read Science

Compare and Contrast

When you **compare** things, you tell how they are alike. When you **contrast** things, you tell how they are different.

- Words such as *similar, like, all, both,* or *in the same way* are clues that things are being compared.
- Words such as *different, unlike,* or *in a different way* are clues that things are being contrasted.

Science Article

Worm Tunnels

Soil in which earthworms live is not like other soil. Earthworms dig tunnels in soil. As a result, plants grow in a different way.

Plant roots grow more quickly down tunnels. Rainwater and air that roots need move easily through them too. Also, earthworms leave body wastes in tunnels. These have a lot of nutrients that plants need to grow.

Unlike soil with worms, soil without earthworms cannot support plants as well.

Apply It!

Study the graphic organizer below.

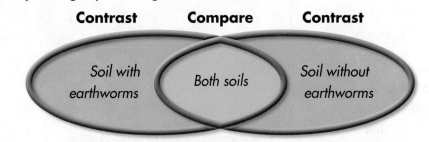

Contrast   Compare   Contrast

Soil with earthworms   Both soils   Soil without earthworms

Make a graphic organizer like the one shown. Use it to **classify** ways that these two soils are alike and different.

You are walking through a lush, green forest. A soft cushion of needles keeps your footsteps silent. You smell the trees. You hear chipmunks twittering in the branches. Birds dart back and forth. This is a beautiful place. But the trees may soon be cut down for lumber and paper. Can we keep our forests and still have the products we need?

Lesson 1

What are resources?

Everything we use comes from materials found on Earth. Some of these materials can be replaced, but others cannot. Some resources are never used up.

Resources That Can Be Replaced

The things we need come from natural resources. A **natural resource** is an important material from the Earth that living things need.

Trees are a natural resource. People cut down trees for wood. Wood is used to build new houses. Wood chips are turned into pulp. Pulp is made into paper. Paper products include boxes, newspapers, and books.

People can plant new trees to replace those cut down. If the new trees get the sunlight, air, and water they need, they can grow big enough to be cut down. A resource that can be replaced in a fairly short time is called a **renewable resource.** Trees are a renewable resource.

These logs at a lumber or paper mill came from trees.

Lumber mills saw tree trunks into boards that are used to build new houses.

1. ✓**Checkpoint** What makes some resources renewable?

2. **Writing in Science** **Expository** In your **science journal** make a table with two columns. Title one column *Wood.* Title the other *Paper.* Use the table to list things found in your home made from each. Then, write two paragraphs about how your family uses wood and paper products.

247

Resources That Cannot Be Replaced

Many natural resources come from below the ground. Miners dig into the ground to get rocks called ores. Ores contain metals and other minerals that people use. Copper, iron, and aluminum are some useful metals. Hematite is an ore that contains the metal iron.

Steel is made from iron. Steel is used to make nails, cars, and many other products. There is only so much iron ore in the ground. Once we use it up, it cannot be replaced. A resource that cannot be replaced is a **nonrenewable resource.**

Coal is a nonrenewable resource. Like oil and natural gas, coal is a fuel. When it is burned it releases useful energy. The energy from these fuels can be used to heat buildings. The energy can power cars and planes. We can get more fuel by digging more of these materials from the ground. But supplies of these fuels are limited.

Using Resources	
Resource	**Uses**
Oil	Gasoline, paint, plastic, shampoo
Coal	Electricity, heat, paint thinner, insecticides
Iron ore	Machines, bicycles, autos, buildings

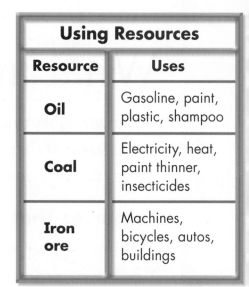

This derrick pumps oil from underground. Some of the oil is made into gasoline for cars.

248

When we use up an ore, mineral, or fuel resource in one place, we must find them in a new place. Mining and drilling can leave permanent marks, such as the open pit mine in the picture. Getting natural resources from Earth can change its surface.

Hematite is an ore that contains iron.

An Endless Supply of Resources

Some natural resources are not used up. Plants need sunlight, air, and water to grow. We need air to breathe and water to drink. These resources are not used up. Sunlight, air, and water are resources that are always available on Earth.

This coal formed in the Earth from plants that lived millions of years ago.

A huge crane loads coal into a dump truck at a mine.

✔ Lesson Checkpoint

1. List two nonrenewable resources.

2. Why is coal a nonrenewable resource?

3. **Compare and Contrast**
   How are renewable and nonrenewable resources alike? How are they different?

249

Dirty water is piped into a wetland in Florida. It will become clean enough to be piped back into a river.

Water from homes is filtered through sand in ponds like these. Farmers use the recycled water for their orange trees.

How can we protect our resources?

We must protect natural resources by not using them up or damaging them.

Using Resources Responsibly

When people walk instead of riding in a car, they save fuel. When they choose products that have less packaging, they save paper and plastic. There is less garbage. Saving in these ways is called conservation. **Conservation** is the wise use of natural resources so that people do not waste them or use them up.

Conserving Water

You can conserve water by using less of it. You can turn off the water while brushing your teeth and take shorter showers.

One way that communities conserve water is to clean used water. Wetlands can clean used water. First, the dirty water is piped into wetlands. Soil filters out harmful particles. Then, plants and tiny living things break down the particles. Finally, the water is clean enough to flow back into a river and be used again.

Conserving Soil

Soil needs protection from erosion. Some farmers plant crops around hills instead of up and down the hills. The curved rows of plants hold back rainwater. Soil soaks up water instead of being washed away. Farmers also plant trees by fields to keep soil from blowing away.

As people in cities need more room, they often build new houses on nearby farmland. Buildings and roads cover the soil. There is less farmland. Landfills may also take up famland space.

We can conserve soil in our own yards. We can put yard clippings and leaves where they decay instead of sending them to a landfill. The decayed material turns into compost. You can add compost to garden soil for fertilizer.

We could allow these leaves to decay into compost. Then they would add nutrients to soil.

Contour plowing keeps soil from washing away.

1. **✓ Checkpoint** Describe ways people can conserve water.

2. **Writing in Science** **Expository** Research ways to make a compost pile that will become fertilizer. In your **science journal** write a paragraph to explain it.

Using Up Land Space for Trash

Everything we use is made from natural resources. For example, plastic milk jugs are made from oil. Food cans are made from metals such as steel and tin. When we no longer need these products, we throw them away. They become trash. The trouble with our trash is that it never really goes away. A truck often hauls trash to a landfill. A landfill is a large area in which trash is buried. Trash rests on top of a liner so that pollution does not leak into groundwater. Once in place, we no longer have to see, smell, or worry about our garbage making us sick. But it still exists and the landfills continue to grow.

We put more than two hundred million tons of trash each year into landfills like this one.

What is in a Year's Worth of My Trash?	
Materials	**Mass (in kilograms)**
Paper	250
Plastic	80
Metal (steel cans)	40
Metal (aluminum cans)	10
Glass	40
Food scraps	80

Landfills are filling up and closing down. The number of landfills has fallen from 8,000 in 1988 to less than 2,000 today. Our need for land in which to bury our trash continues to grow. Most people, however, would rather see land used for other purposes.

One way we are reducing the need for landfill space is by burning garbage in special furnaces. Burning garbage also gives off energy that can heat buildings and generate electricity. However, the smoke from the burning must be cleaned. If the smoke is not cleaned, it can harm the air we breathe. Special smoke cleaners are expensive.

Another way we are lessening the need for landfill space is by reducing the amount of trash we make. If we were not doing this, we would have needed 100 new landfill areas. What are ways we are reducing the amount of trash we make?

These are objects we use every day. Can some of these materials be used again?

✓ Lesson Checkpoint

1. Where does most garbage go after it is taken from your home?

2. What are some ways to save landfill space?

3. **Math in Science** If you throw away 2 kilograms of trash each day, how much trash would you throw away in a year?

What are ways to use resources again?

Many things can be used more than once. Old materials can be used to make new things. Reusing and recycling conserves land, keeping it from becoming landfill space.

Using Resources Again

When you reuse things, you conserve resources. For example, you can reuse cloth napkins, but not paper ones. You can reuse empty jars to store leftover food. Or you can give toys and clothes you have outgrown to others to use.

Another way to conserve resources is to recycle things that contain useful material. You **recycle** when you change something so that it can be used again. The useful resources that went into making objects can then be made into new products. Many of these new products are made from recycled metal, glass, plastic, or paper.

Sort Glass
Recycled glass bottles and jars are separated by color. They are broken into small pieces.

Ship to Glass Company
Pieces of glass are put into boxes. The boxes are shipped to a glass reprocessing company.

Let's follow the process used to recycle things that contain glass. Workers at the recycling plant sort glass by color. Common colors are clear, brown, and green. The bottles and jars are then broken into pieces called shards. Shards are shipped to glass companies. Glass shards must be passed under a magnet to remove metal caps and rings. Shards are then crushed into grain-sized particles called cullet. The cullet is cleaned and dried. Now the cullet is ready to be turned into new glass things. It is melted in furnaces and blown by machines into glass bottles and jars. Some is flattened into windowpanes. If glass is recycled, it can be used over and over again.

1. ✅ **Checkpoint** What are the four main types of materials that are recycled?

2. 🎯 **Compare and Contrast** How is recycling glass the same as recycling water? How does recycling glass differ from recycling water?

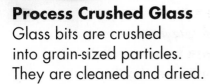

Process Crushed Glass
Glass bits are crushed into grain-sized particles. They are cleaned and dried.

Make New Glass Bottles
The bits are melted and reformed into glass bottles or jars.

Saving Energy

100-watt light bulb

Food can

Glass bottle

It takes more energy to make new steel cans and glass bottles than to recycle them. Recycling one soup can may save enough energy to light a 100-watt bulb for about half an hour. Recycling one glass bottle saves enough energy for four hours of light.

This park bench was made from recycled plastic. It will last for about 50 years.

This wall is made of old tires and aluminum cans held together with mud and straw.

A reused plastic barrel makes a terrific flower pot.

Using Recycled Materials

Reusing and recycling are not new ideas. Your great-grandparents might have bought flour in cloth sacks. They cleaned the empty sacks, cut them, and sewed them into rags, towels, and even clothing!

Today, recycling is easier than ever. Many communities collect items to be recycled when they collect the regular garbage. Places such as movie theaters and office buildings have special containers for bottles and cans. Grocery stores collect used plastic shopping bags that can be recycled.

Conserving recycled material requires buying or using products that include it. For example, you can shop for products made out of recycled material. Your next sleeping bag might include stuffing made out of shredded plastic bottles. Your next sweater might be knit out of yarn recycled from old garments. Or you can play on playgrounds that have a surface made out of shredded car tires.

This playhouse was made from recycled plastic milk bottles.

The Three *R's*

What's a good way to remember what you've learned to protect natural resources? Just think about the three *R's*—reduce, reuse, and recycle. *Reduce* the amount of resources you use and the trash you make. *Reuse* old things in new ways. *Recycle* everything you can. Every time you practice one of the three *R's*, you are helping to care for Earth.

Stuffing in this sleeping bag and yarn in this sweater are from recycled materials.

✔ **Lesson Checkpoint**

1. Why is it important to recycle?

2. What are the three *R's*?

3. **Art in Science** Draw or make a model showing how you might reuse something in an unusual way.

257

Recycling

Almost everything we throw away can be recycled. But we do a better job recycling some things than other things.

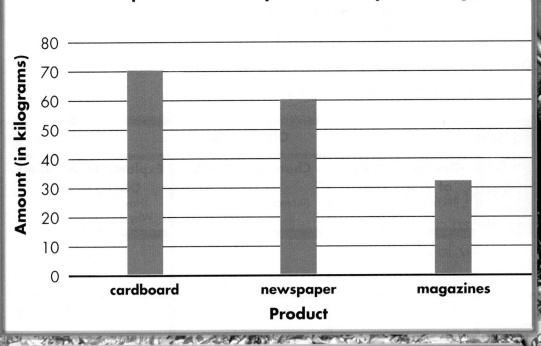

Amount of Paper Products Recycled for Every 100 Kilograms

Amount (in kilograms)

80
70
60
50
40
30
20
10
0

cardboard   newspaper   magazines

Product

The bar graph shows how much of three different paper products we recycle. We recycle 70 kilograms of cardboard boxes from every 100 kilograms we make. We recycle 60 kilograms of newspapers from every 100 kilograms we make. But we recycle only 32 kilograms of magazines from every 100 kilograms we make.

Cans and Bottles Recycled for Every 100 Kilograms Made

Amount (in kilograms)

80
60
40
20
0

steel cans | aluminum cans | plastic soft-drink bottles | plastic milk bottles | glass containers

Product

This bar graph shows how many kilograms of cans and bottles we recycle from every 100 kilograms we make.

Use the graph to answer the questions.

1 About how many kilograms of glass containers do we recycle from every 100 kilograms made?

A. about 58 kilograms

B. about 32 kilograms

C. about 28 kilograms

D. about 22 kilograms

2 Which container is recycled most?

F. steel cans

G. aluminum cans

H. plastic soft drink bottles

I. plastic milk bottles

3 From every 100 kilograms of aluminum cans we make, about how many kilograms do we **not** recycle?

A. about 50 kilograms

B. about 20 kilograms

C. about 80 kilograms

D. about 100 kilograms

Lab zone **Take-Home Activity**

Recycling 1 glass jar saves enough energy to run a TV for 3 hours. Find how many glass jars you have in your kitchen. How many hours of TV-watching in your home would recycling the jars pay for in energy savings?

Chapter 9 Review and Test Prep

Use Vocabulary

conservation (page 250)	**recycle** (page 254)
natural resource (page 247)	**renewable resource** (page 247)
nonrenewable resource (page 248)	

Use the term from the list above that best completes each sentence.

1. Trees, iron ore, water, and air are each a _____.

2. A natural resource that can be replaced in a fairly short period of time is a _____.

3. When we change something so it can be used again, we _____ it.

4. A resource that cannot be replaced once it is used up is a _____.

5. The saving and wise use of Earth's resources is called _____.

Explain Concepts

6. Explain the difference between a renewable resource like trees and a nonrenewable resource like iron ore.

7. What is the difference between a limited resource like iron ore and a limitless resource like air?

8. What are ways to conserve soil?

9. How is making compost out of yard wastes and food scraps one solution to the garbage problem?

10. Why is conserving natural resources important to everyone?

11. Why should people try to buy products made from recycled materials?

Process Skills

12. We get milk from cows and wool to make clothing from sheep. **Infer** whether milk and wool are renewable or nonrenewable resources. Explain your answer.

13. Copy the table below on a sheet of paper. Then **classify** each kind of trash as paper, plastic, or metal.

Trash	Classification
Milk carton	
Soft-drink can	
Magazine	
Laundry detergent bottle	

Compare and Constrast

14. Make a graphic organizer like the one below. Write in each part ways to show how reusing and recycling are similar and different.

Both
Reusing   **Reusing/ Recycling**   **Recycling**

Test Prep

Choose the letter that best completes the statement or answers the question.

15. Which of the following is a renewable resource?

Ⓐ coal   Ⓑ oil
Ⓒ aluminum   Ⓓ sunlight

16. Which of the following does NOT conserve soil?

Ⓕ planting different crops
Ⓖ planting trees along the edges of fields
Ⓗ plowing up and down hillsides
Ⓘ adding compost to soil

17. Which of the following is a nonrenewable resource?

Ⓐ soil
Ⓑ iron ore
Ⓒ water
Ⓓ trees

18. Many power plants use coal to make electricity. Which of the following is a way you could help conserve coal?

Ⓕ Ride a bicycle instead of riding in a car.
Ⓖ Leave the television on when going outside.
Ⓗ Turn off lights when leaving a room.
Ⓘ Plant a flower garden using compost.

19. Explain why the answer you selected for Question 18 is best. For each of the answers you do not select, give a reason why it is not the best choice.

20. Writing in Science

Narrative Write a story about a person who saw how natural resources were not being protected and did something about it.

Recycling Plant Worker

Workers sort paper to be recycled.

Recycled paper has become a roll of paper to be used again.

Many people work to conserve our natural resources. They have many different kinds of jobs. This is just one of them. But remember, conserving resources is a job you can do every day by using resources wisely.

Workers at recycling plants do their part to battle the garbage problem. Some work at plants that recycle aluminum or steel. Some workers drive trucks that pick up metals and take them to the plant. At the plant, other workers operate machines that shred the metal into small pieces. Still other workers melt and reshape the metal into new products.

Most recycling plant workers need at least a high school education.

Lab zone Take-Home Activity

Paper, aluminum and steel cans, and plastic are recyclable. List the steps you take or would take to recycle these materials in your home.

Unit B Test Talk

Choose the Right Answer

To answer a multiple-choice test question, you need to choose an answer from several choices. Read the passage and then answer the questions.

> **Evaporation** changes water to an invisible gas called water vapor. **Condensation** changes water vapor into tiny drops of liquid water. These processes are parts of the water cycle.
>
> Water also causes **weathering** by breaking rocks into smaller pieces. Water then carries the weathered rock to different places.
>
> There is always the same amount of water on Earth. However, it is important to conserve fresh water and not waste it.

Use What You Know

To choose the right answer, eliminate answer choices that you are sure are incorrect.

1. In the passage, the word "condensation" means
   (A) liquid water changes into water vapor.
   (B) water vapor changes into liquid water.
   (C) liquid water changes into solid ice.
   (D) solid ice changes into liquid water.

2. In the passage, the word "weathering" means
   (F) causing weather patterns.
   (G) changing water vapor into clouds.
   (H) carrying pieces of rock to different places.
   (I) breaking rocks into smaller pieces.

3. Which of the following statements about water is true?
   (A) The amount of Earth's water always changes.
   (B) Water can change Earth's surface.
   (C) Condensation changes liquid water to water vapor.
   (D) Evaporation changes water vapor to liquid water.

Unit B Wrap-Up

Chapter 5

How does water change form?

- Living things need water to survive. People use water in many ways.
- Heating and cooling changes water between the forms of liquid, solid, and gas.

Chapter 6

How does weather follow patterns?

- Ways in which the sun heats the Earth and influences the water cycle cause weather patterns.
- Knowing about weather patterns helps people predict the weather and be safe.

Chapter 7

What are some kinds of rocks and soils?

- Rocks differ on the basis of how they form and what minerals they are made of.
- Soil covers most of Earth's land and is made of bits of rock, water, and humus.

Chapter 8

How do forces cause changes on Earth's surface?

- Forces within the Earth cause volcanoes and earthquakes to change Earth's surface quickly.
- Earth's surface can be changed slowly or sometimes quickly by weathering and erosion.

Chapter 9

How can people use natural resources responsibly?

● People can plant trees to replace ones they cut down and do things to make soil healthy and useful again.

● People can conserve natural resources by reducing the amount of resources they use and trash they make. They can also reuse and recycle materials.

Performance Assessment

Identify Changing Forms of Water

Water can be a solid, a liquid, or a gas. What changing forms of water can you identify? Place ice cubes and water in a plastic cup. Put the cup in a warm place and observe it over time. What forms of water were in the cup when you started? How did the forms change?

Read More About Earth Science!

Look for books like these in the library.

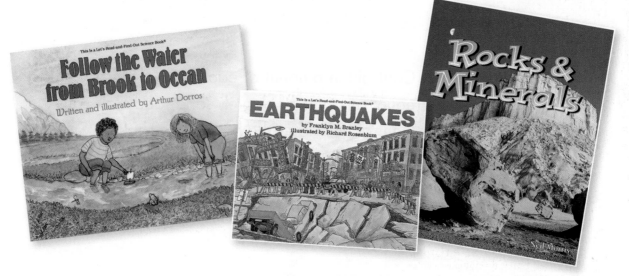

Experiment What settles first?

As a river flows to an ocean, it can carry particles of soil. The soil particles may be small, large, or in between. Some of them may settle out of the water quickly and are not carried far. Some may settle out of the water very slowly. These may be carried a long distance.

Materials

3 small measuring cups

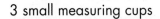

small gravel, sand, clay soil

hand lens

plastic bottles with caps

funnel and water

Process Skills

Experiments have a **variable** you change, a variable you **observe**, and variables you **control**.

Ask a question.

How do particles in water settle out?

State a hypothesis.

If particles are larger, then do those particles settle faster, slower, or at about the same speed as smaller particles? Write your **hypothesis**.

Identify and control variables.

The **variable** you change is the size of the particles. The variable you **observe** is how fast the particles settle. Every other part of the experiment must be **controlled**, or kept the same.

Control the amount of each type of particle. Use equal amounts of gravel, sand, and clay soil. Control how long the bottles are shaken. Shake all bottles the same length of time. Control when the particles start to settle. Stop shaking all the bottles at the same time.

Test your hypothesis.

1 **Measure** 30 mL of gravel, 30 mL of sand, and 30 mL of clay soil. Observe the particles. Use a hand lens. Observe their size, shape, and color. In a chart, record their sizes (smallest, medium-sized, largest).

2 Put each kind of particle into a different bottle. Use a funnel. Fill each bottle $\frac{3}{4}$ full with water.

3 Screw the caps on tightly. **Predict** which particles will settle out fastest. Along with 2 others in your group, begin shaking the bottles.

Hint: If the funnel jams, tap it or shake it.

gravel

sand

clay soil

$\frac{3}{4}$ full with water

④ At the same time, stop shaking the bottles.
Put them on a table. Observe what happens.

⑤ Record the order in which the contents settle.

⑥ Repeat twice. Do a total of 3 trials. Compare your results
with your prediction and with those of other groups.

Collect and record your data.

Type of Particles	Size of Particles (smallest, medium-sized, largest)
Small gravel	
Sand	
Clay soil	

More Lab zone Activities Take It to the Net
pearsonsuccessnet.com

Interpret your data.

Complete the charts. Analyze the information. Compare the sizes of the particles and how fast they settle.

Type of Particles	Speed of Settling (fastest, medium, slowest)				
	Predicted	Trial A	Trial B	Trial C	Overall
Small gravel					
Sand					
Clay soil					

Why do you think scientists repeat experiments?

Type of Particles	Size of Particles (smallest, medium-sized, largest)	Speed of Settling (fastest, medium, slowest)
Small gravel		
Sand		
Clay soil		

State your conclusion.

Cooperate with others in your group. Discuss your results. Consider the explanations of others. Respect their ideas. Draw a conclusion from your data. Does it agree with your hypothesis?

Communicate your conclusion.

Go Further

What would happen if soil particles of different sizes were mixed together? Make a prediction based on the results of this activity. Design and carry out a plan to investigate.

Full Inquiry

Using Scientific Methods

1. Ask a question.
2. State your hypothesis.
3. Identify/control variables.
4. Test your hypothesis.
5. Collect and record your data.
6. Interpret your data.
7. State your conclusion.
8. Go further.

Predicting Weather

Weather patterns help people predict the weather, but predictions can be wrong.

Idea: Compare your observations of the weather with weather forecasts from TV and radio stations, and newspapers to see how accurate they are.

Comparing Soils

Soils have different amounts of sand, silt, clay, and humus.

Idea: Use a hand lens to compare soil samples in your area.

An Earthquake Model

Most earthquakes happen along breaks in Earth's crust.

Idea: Use clay, heavy cardboard, and objects to model what happens to Earth's crust, roads, and other objects during an earthquake.

Recycling

Recycling conserves landfill space and resources.

Idea: Use information about your community's recycling program to make a display with examples of what can be recycled and ways to sort it.

EC CRII 10 9 8 7 6 5 4 3 2 1

Metric and Customary Measurement

The metric system is the measurement system most commonly used in science. Metric units are sometimes called SI units. SI stands for International System because these units are used around the world.

These prefixes are used in the metric system:

kilo- means *thousand*
1 kilometer equals 1,000 meters
centi- means *hundredths*
100 centimeters equals 1 meter
milli- means one-*thousandth*
1,000 millimeters equals 1 meter

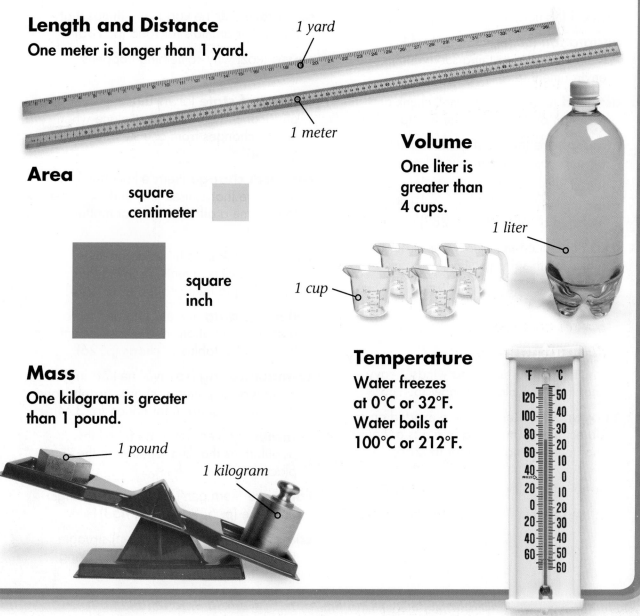

Length and Distance
One meter is longer than 1 yard.

1 yard

1 meter

Area

square centimeter

square inch

Volume
One liter is greater than 4 cups.

1 liter

1 cup

Mass
One kilogram is greater than 1 pound.

1 pound

1 kilogram

Temperature
Water freezes at 0°C or 32°F. Water boils at 100°C or 212°F.

Glossary

The glossary uses letters and signs to show how words are pronounced. The mark ′ is placed after a syllable with a primary or heavy accent. The mark ′ is placed after a syllable with a secondary or lighter accent.

To hear these words pronounced, listen to the AudioText CD.

Pronunciation Key

a	in hat	ō	in open	sh	in she
ā	in age	ȯ	in all	th	in thin
â	in care	ô	in order	ŦH	in then
ä	in far	oi	in oil	zh	in measure
e	in let	ou	in out	ə	= a in about
ē	in equal	u	in cup	ə	= e in taken
ėr	in term	u̇	in put	ə	= i in pencil
i	in it	ü	in rule	ə	= o in lemon
ī	in ice	ch	in child	ə	= u in circus
o	in hot	ng	in long		

absorb (ab sôrb′) to take in (p. 373)

adaptation (ad′ ap tā′ shən) trait that helps a living thing survive in its environment (p. 48)

asteroid (as′tə roid′) a small chunk of rock that orbits around the Sun (p. 457)

atmosphere (at′mə sfir) the blanket of air and gases that surround the Earth (p. 176)

atom (at′əm) one of the tiny particles that make up all of matter (p. 282)

axis (ak′sis) an imaginary line around which Earth spins (p. 424)

blizzard (bliz′ərd) a winter storm with very low temperatures, strong winds, heavy snowfall, and blowing snow (p. 183)

buoyancy (boi′ən sē) force exerted on an object that is immersed in a gas or liquid that tends to make it float (p. 286)

carnivore (kär′nə vôr) living things that hunt other animals for food (p. 106)

cause (kȯz) why something happens (p. 277, 311)

change of state (chānj uv stāt) physical change that takes place when matter changes from one state to another (p. 304)

chemical change (kem′ə kəl chānj) a change that causes one kind of matter to become a different kind of matter (p. 311)

classifying (klas′ə fī′ing) to arrange or sort objects, events, or living things according to their properties (p. 244)

collecting data (kə lek′ ting dā′ tə) to gather observations and measurements into graphs, tables or charts (p. 26)

communicating (kə myü′ nə kāt′ ing) using words, pictures, charts, graphs, and diagrams to share information (p. 324)

community (kəm myü′ nə tē) all the populations that live together in the same place (p. 74)

compare (kəm pâr′) to show how things are alike (p. 5, 245, 389, 453)

competition (kom′ pə tish′ən) struggle that happens when two or more living things need the same resource (p. 110)

compression wave (kəm presh′ən wāv) wave that has spaces where particles are squeezed together and spaces where particles are spread apart (p. 396)

computer (kəm pyü′ tər) tool which stores, processes, and gets electronic information (p. 485)

conclusion (kən klü′ zhən) decision reached after considering facts and details (p. 101)

condensation (kon′ den sā′ shən) the changing of a gas into a liquid (p. 157)

coniferous tree (kō nif′ər əs trē) a tree that produces seeds in cones (p. 16)

conservation (kon′ sər vā′ shən) wise use of natural resources (p. 250)

constellation (kon′ stə lā′ shən) a group of stars that make a pattern (p. 438)

consumer (kən sü′ mər) living things that eat food (p. 106)

contrast (kən trast′) to show how things are different (p. 5, 245, 389, 453)

core (kôr) the innermost layer of Earth (p. 223)

crust (krust) the outermost layer of Earth (p. 223)

decay (di kā′) to break down, or rot (p. 118, 206)

deciduous (di sij′ü əs) loses leaves in fall and grows new ones in spring (p. 14)

decomposer (dē′kəm pō′zər) a living thing that breaks down waste and things that have died (p. 118)

density (den′sə tē) measure of the amount of matter in a certain amount of space (p. 286)

desert (dez′ərt) an ecosystem that gets less than 25 cm of rainfall a year (p. 78)

details (di tālz′) individual pieces of information that support a main idea (p. 69, 357)

disease (də zēz′) the name we give an illness (p. 126)

dwarf planet (dwôrf plan′it) small, ball-shaped object that revolves around the Sun (p. 465)

earthquake (ėrth′kwāk′) a shaking of Earth's crust caused by sudden, shifting movements in the crust (p. 228)

ecosystem (ē′kō sis′təm) all the living and nonliving things that interact with each other in a given area (p. 72)

effect (ə fekt′) what happens as the result of a cause (p. 149, 277)

electric charge (i lek′trik chärj) tiny amount of energy in the particles of matter (p. 374)

electric circuit (i lek′trik sėr′kit) the path that a controlled electric current flows through (p. 376)

electric current (i lek′trik kėr′ənt) the movement of an electric charge from one place to another (p. 376)

element (el′ə mənt) matter that has only one kind of atom (p. 282)

energy (en′ ər jē) the ability to do work or to cause a change (p. 359)

environment (en vī′rən mənt) everything that surrounds a living thing (p. 71)

equator (i kwā′ tər) the imaginary line that separates the north and south halves of Earth (p. 429)

erosion (i rō′ zhən) the movement of weathered materials (p. 232)

estimating and measuring (es′tə māt ing and mezh′ər ing) to tell what you think an object's measurements are and then to measure it in units (p. 210)

evaporation (i vap′ ə rā′ shən) the changing of a liquid into a gas (p. 157)

experiment (ek sper′ə ment) to formulate and test a hypothesis using a scientific method (p. 140)

explore (ek splôr′) to study a scientific idea in a hands-on manner (p. 36)

extinct (ek stingkt′) no longer lives on Earth (p. 23)

food chain (füd chān) the movement of energy from one type of living thing to another (p. 108)

food web (füd web) the flow of energy between food chains which ties a community together (p. 108)

force (fôrs) a push or a pull (p. 332)

forming questions and hypotheses (fôrm′ing kwes′chənz and hī poth′ə sēz′) to think of how you can solve a problem or answer a question (p. 140)

fossil (fos′ əl) remains or mark of a living thing from long ago (p. 22)

friction (frik′ shən) a contact force that opposes the motion of an object (p. 333)

gas (gas) the form of matter which has no shape, has particles that are not connected to each other, and takes up whatever space is available (p. 281)

germinate (jėr′ mə nāt) begins to grow (p. 20)

germs (jėrmz) small living things that include bacteria and viruses, many of which can cause illness (p. 126)

grassland (gras′ land′) land ecosystem that has many grasses and few trees (p. 76)

gravity (grav′ə tē) a non-contact force that pulls objects toward each other (p. 336)

groundwater (ground′ wȯ′ tər) water that has slowly made its way through soil and then collects in spaces between underground rock; it is brought to the surface by digging wells (p. 155)

habitat (hab′ə tat) the place where a living thing makes its home (p. 72)

heat (hēt) the transfer of thermal energy from one piece of matter to another (p. 366)

herbivore (ėr′bə vôr) living things that eat only plants (p. 106)

hibernate (hī′bər nāt) to spend winter resting; body systems slow down in order to save energy (p. 52)

hurricane (hėr′ə kān) a huge, strong storm that forms over the ocean (p. 182)

identifying and controlling variables (ī den′tə fī ing and kən trōl′ ing vâr′ē ə bəlz) to change one thing, but keep all the other factors the same (p. 40)

igneous rock (ig′nē əs rok′) rock that forms when melted earth materials cool and harden (p. 200)

inclined plane (in klīnd′ plān) a slanting surface that connects a lower level to a higher level (p. 340)

inference (in′fər əns) a conclusion based on facts, experiences, observations, or knowledge (p. 173)

inferring (in fėr′ ing) to draw a conclusion or make a reasonable guess based on what you have learned or what you know (p. 100)

inherited (in her′it əd) passed on from parent to offspring (p. 48)

interpreting data (in tėr′prit ing dā′tə) to use the information you have collected to solve problems or answer questions (p. 26)

invention (in ven′ shən) something that has been made for the first time (p. 479)

investigate (in ves′ tə gāt) to solve a problem or answer a question by following an existing procedure or an original one (p. 26)

investigating and experimenting (in ves′ tə gāt ing and ek sper′ə ment ing) to plan and do an investigation to test a hypothesis or solve a problem (p. 508)

kinetic energy (ki net′ik en′ər jē) energy of motion (p. 361)

landform (land′ fôrm) a natural feature on the surface of Earth's crust (p. 224)

larva (lär′ və) stage in an insect's life after it hatches from the egg (p. 45)

lava (lä′ və) hot, molten rock on Earth's surface (p. 226)

lever (lev′ər) a simple machine used to lift and move things (p. 341)

life cycle (līf sī′kəl) the stages through which an organism passes between birth and death (p. 44)

light (līt) a form of energy that can be seen (p. 370)

liquid (lik′wid) matter that does not have a definite shape but takes up a definite amount of space (p. 280)

loam (lōm) soil that contains a mixture of humus and mineral materials of sand, silt, and clay (p. 209)

lunar eclipse (lü′nər i klips′) Earth's shadow moving across the Moon (p. 434)

magma (mag′mə) hot, molten rock that forms deep underground (p. 226)

magnetic (mag net′ik) having the property to pull on, or attract, metals that have iron in them (p. 337)

magnetism (mag′nə tiz′əm) a non-contact force that pulls objects containing iron (p. 337)

main idea (mān ī dē′ə) what a paragraph is about; the most important idea (p. 69, 357)

making operational definitions (māk′ ing op′ə rā′ shən əl def′ə nish′ənz) to define or describe an object or event based on your own experience (p. 68)

making and using models (māk′ ing and yüz′ ing mod′lz) to make a model from materials or to make a sketch or a diagram (p. 36)

mantle (man′tl) the middle layer of Earth (p. 223)

mass (mas) amount of matter (p. 284)

matter (mat′ər) anything that takes up space and has mass (p. 279)

metamorphic rock (met′ ə môr′ fik rok′) rock that forms when existing rock is changed by heat and pressure (p. 200)

microscopic (mī′krə skop′ ik) not able to be seen without a microscope (p. 126)

migrate (mī′ grāt) to move to another place to find better climate, food, or a mate (p. 52)

mineral (min′ ər əl) natural material that forms from nonliving matter (p. 199)

mixture (miks′ chər) two or more kinds of matter that are placed together but can be easily separated (p. 306)

Moon (mün) the natural satellite that orbits around Earth (p. 432)

Moon phase (mün fāz) the way the Moon looks because of the amount of the lit side of the Moon that can be seen from Earth at the same time (p. 434)

motion (mō′shən) a change in the position of an object (p. 327)

natural resources (nach′ ər əl ri sôrs′əz) natural materials, such as soil, wood, water, air, oil, or minerals, that living things need (p. 247)

nonrenewable resources (non ri nü′ə bəl ri sôrs′ əz) resource that cannot be replaced once it is used up (p. 248)

nutrient (nü′ trē ənt) thing plants need in order to grow (p. 206)

observing (əb zėrv′ ing) using your senses to find out about objects, events, or living things (p. 4)

omnivore (om′ nə vôr′) living things that eat plants and other animals for food (p. 106)

orbit (ôr′ bit) the path of any object in space that revolves around another object in space (p. 456)

organ (ôr′ gən) a structure containing different tissues that are organized to carry out a specific function of the body such as a stomach, intestine, etc. (p. 123)

periodic table (pir′ē od′ik tā′bəl) an arrangement of elements based on their properties (p. 283)

physical change (fiz′ ə kəl chānj) a change that makes matter look different without becoming a new substance (p. 303)

pitch (pich) how high or low a sound is (p. 392)

planet (plan′it) a large, ball-shaped body of matter that revolves, or travels, around any star (p. 456)

pollinate (pol′ ə nāt) move pollen from the part of a flower that makes pollen to the part of a flower that makes seeds (p. 15)

pollution (pə lü′ shən) waste materials that make the environment dirty (p. 124)

population (pop′ yə lā′ shən) all the living things of the same kind that live in the same place at the same time (p. 74)

position (pə zish′ ən) the location of an object (p. 327)

potential energy (pə ten′shəl en′ ər jē) the energy something has because of its position (p. 360)

precipitation (pri sip′ə tā′ shən) water that falls to Earth as rain, hail, sleet, or snow (p. 159)

predator (pred′ə tər) a consumer that hunts other animals for food (p. 107)

predicting (pri dikt′ ing) to tell what you think will happen (p. 162)

pressure (presh′ər) force per unit area that is applied to a substance (p. 281)

prey (prā) any animal that is hunted by others for food (p. 107)

producer (prə dü′sər) living things that make their own food (p. 106)

property (prop′ər tē) something about matter that you can observe with one or more of your senses (p. 279)

pulley (pu̇l′ē) a machine that changes the direction of motion of an object to which a force is applied (p. 343)

pupa (pyü′pə) stage in an insect's life between larva and adult (p. 45)

R

recycle (rē sī′kəl) treat or process something so it can be used again (p. 254)

reflect (ri flekt′) to bounce off of (p. 372)

refract (ri frakt′) to bend (p. 372)

relative position (rel′ə tiv pə zish′ən) a change in an object's position compared to another object (p. 329)

renewable resource (ri nü′ ə bəl ri sôrs′) resource that is endless like sunlight, or that is naturally replaced in a fairly short time, such as trees (p. 247)

resource (ri sôrs′) See Natural Resources, Renewable Resources, Nonrenewable Resources

revolution (rev′ə lü′ shən) one complete trip around the Sun (p. 428)

rock (rok) natural, solid, nonliving material made of one or more minerals (p. 199)

rotation (rō tā′ shən) one complete spin on an axis (p. 425)

S

scientific method (sī′ən tif′ik meth′əd) organized ways of finding answers and solving problems (p. xxvi)

sedimentary rock (sed′ə men′tər ē rok′) rock that forms when small pieces of earth materials collect and become bound together (p. 200)

seed leaf (sēd lēf) part of a seed that has stored food (p. 20)

seedling (sēd′ ling) a new, small plant that grows from a seed (p. 20)

sequence (sē′kwəns) the order in which events take place (p. 37, 221, 421, 477)

soil (soil) the part of Earth's surface consisting of humus and weathered rock in which plants grow (p. 206)

solar system (sō′lər sis′təm) the Sun, eight planets and their moons, dwarf planets, and other objects that revolve around the Sun (p. 456)

solid (sol′id) matter that has a definite shape and takes up a definite amount of space (p. 280)

solution (sə lü′shən) a mixture in which one or more substances dissolves in another (p. 308)

speed (spēd) the rate at which an object changes position (p. 330)

star (stär) a massive ball of hot gases that produces its own light (p. 423)

states of matter (stāts uv mat′ər) the forms of matter – solid, liquid, and gas (p. 304)

summarize (sum′ə rīz′) to cover the main ideas or details in a sentence or two (p. 325)

Sun (sun) our star; a huge ball of hot, glowing gases (p. 424)

system (sis′təm) a set of parts that interact with one another (p. 8)

T

technology (tek nol′ə jē) the use of science knowledge to invent tools and new ways of doing things (p. 479)

telescope (tel′ə skōp) a tool that gathers lots of light and magnifies objects that are far away and makes faint stars easier to see (p. 436)

thermal energy (thėr′məl en′ər jē) the total kinetic energy of all the particles that make up matter (p. 366)

tool (tül) an object used to do work (p. 479)

tornado (tôr nā′ dō) a rotating column of air that touches the ground and causes damage with its high winds (p. 182)

trait (trāt) a feature passed on to a living thing from its parents (p. 40)

tundra (tun′drə) land ecosystem that is cold and dry (p. 80)

vertebrate (ver′tə brit) animal with a backbone (p. 40)

vibration (vī brā′shən) a very quick back-and-forth movement (p. 392)

volcano (vol kā′nō) an opening in the Earth's crust from which hot, melted material erupts (p. 226)

volume (vol′yəm) amount of space matter takes up (p. 285)

water cycle (wȯ′tər sī′kəl) the movement of water from Earth's surface into the air and back again (p. 158)

water vapor (wȯ′tər vā′pər) water in the form of an invisible gas in the air (p. 154)

weather (weᴛʜ′ər) what it is like outside including temperature, wind, clouds, and precipitation (p. 175)

weathering (weᴛʜ′ər ing) any process that changes rocks by breaking them into smaller pieces (p. 230)

wetland (wet′land′) low land ecosystem that is covered by water at least part of the time during the year; marshes and swamps are wetlands (p. 86)

wheel and axle (wēl and ak′səl) a simple machine made of a wheel and a rod joined to the center of the wheel (p. 342)

work (werk) what happens when a force moves an object over a distance (p. 338)

Index

This index lists the pages on which topics appear in this book. Page numbers after a *p* refer to a photograph or drawing. Page numbers after a *c* refer to a chart, graph, or diagram.

A

Absorb, *p*354, 373

Activities
Directed Inquiry, Explore, 4, 36, 68, 100, 148, 172, 196, 220, 244, 276, 300, 324, 356, 388, 420, 452, 476

Guided Inquiry, Investigate, 26–27, 58–59, 90–91, 128–129, 162–163, 184–185, 210–211, 234–235, 258–259, 290–291, 314–315, 344–345, 378–379, 402–403, 440–441, 466–467, 498–499

Full Inquiry, Experiment, 140–143, 268–271, 412–415, 508–511

Take-Home Activity, 29, 32, 61, 64, 93, 96, 131, 135, 136, 165, 168, 187, 191, 192, 213, 216, 237, 240, 261, 264, 293, 296, 317,320, 347, 351, 352, 381, 384, 405, 408, 443, 447, 448, 469, 472, 501, 504

Adaptation, *p*35, *p*48
animal, 48–53
for getting food, 49, *p*49
for protection, 50, *p*50

Air
clean, 120, *p*121
movement of, 180
plant and animal needs for, 7
safe, 120
sound waves in, 398
speed of sound through, 405, *c*405

Airplane, 477, 497, *p*497
weather and, *p*176
Wright Brothers and, 352, *p*352

Air pollution
from burning fuel, 493
technology and, 481

Air pressure, 177, 178

Air Traffic Controller, 192, *p*192

Alaska, 80

Aldrin, Edwin, 497, *p*497

Algae, 112, *p*112

Alligators, *p*87

Altocumulus clouds, 190

Amber, 55

Ammonites, *p*200

Amphibians, *p*41, 46, *p*46

Anemometer, 177

Anglerfish, 370, *p*370

Animals
adaptations of, *p*48, 48–53, *p*49, *p*50, *p*51
with backbones, 40
without backbones, 42, *p*43
behavior, 52, *p*52
body coverings of, 69
compared with plants, 5
competition among, *p*110

competition for space, 112
coral as, *p*89
desert, 78, *p*79
environmental change and, 114–117
in Everglades, 86, *p*86
in forest ecosystems, *p*83
of grasslands, *p*77
groupings, 40–41
in groups, 104
growth and change, 44–47
homes of, 69
learning, *p*53, 53
needs of, 39, *p*39
from past (fossils), *p*54, 54–57, *p*55, *p*56, *p*57
plant interactions with, *p*98
in saltwater ecosystems, 88, *p*89
seeds scattered by, *p*18
shapes and sizes of, 38
in soil, 212, *p*212, *c*213, *p*213
sounds made by, *p*401
in tropical forest, 84, *p*84
in tundra, 80, *p*81

Apollo 11 Moon landing, 497, *p*497

Aqueducts, 496, *p*496

Aquifer, 258–259, *p*258–259

Arch, 479

Armor of animals, *p*51

Armstrong, Neil, 497, *p*497

Arthropods, *c*42, *p*43

Art in Science, 19, 41, 49, 71, 107, 117, 225, 257, 375, 401, 437, 455, 479

Asteroid, *p*451, 457, *p*462

Asteroid Belt, p457, p462

Astronauts, 134, p134, 350–351, p350–351

Astronomers, 504

Atmosphere, 148, 176, p176, 461
on Earth, 460
of outer planets, 462

Atom, p274, 282, p282

Australian Great Barrier Reef, p89

Axis, p418, 424, p425, 428, p429
seasons and, 430

Backbone
animals with, 40
animals without, 42, p43

Badlands, South Dakota, 56, p57

Baking, 310–311, p310–311

Balance for measuring, 284, p284, p293

Bar Graph, c93, c260–c261

Barnacles, 104, p104

Barometer, 177, p177

Bat, p52

Battery
chemical changes in, p312, 313
chemical energy in, 360, p360

Bear, p107

Beaver, p83, 114, p114

Bee, p104

Behavior of animals, 52, p52

Bell, Alexander Graham, 497

Bicycle
change of motion by, 335, p335
friction and, 334, p335

Big Bear, 438, p438

Big Dipper, 438, p438, 439, p439

Bills, p49

Biography
Jean Dickey, 240
Galileo, 448
Clifton Horne, 408
Elissa R. Levine, 216
Paul Sereno, 64
Eric Stolen, 96
Wright Brothers, 352, p352

Birds, p41, p49, p83

Birth stage, c44

Bison, p77

Blizzard, p171, 183, p183

Blood, 151

Blood vessels, p124, 125

Bobcat, p79

Body
minerals used by, c204
water content of, 151

Boiling, 369

Breathing
by animals, 39
by tadpole, p47

Bridges, 478

Bryce Canyon, Utah, p233

Building materials, 481, p481

Buoyancy, p275, 286, 287, p287

Burning, 311, p311
of fuel, p370
light from, 370
to produce electricity, 493

Butterfly, p44, p52

Cactus, 12, p12, 78

Calcium, 204, c204

California
earthquakes, p228, c236
redwood tree, p73

Calories, c130, 130–131

Camouflage, 50, p51

Carbon dioxide, 8, 184–185

Career
Air Traffic Controller, 192, p192
Astronomer, 504
Chemist, 296
Computer Engineer, 472
Electrical Engineer, 384
Firefighter, 320
Oceanographer, 168
Park Ranger, 136
Plant Researcher, 32
Recycling Plant Worker, 264
Teacher, 504

Caribou, p80

Carnivore, 106

Cast
of fossil, p54

Caterpillar, p44, 45

Cattails, p106

Cause and Effect, 149, 152, 159, 167, 277, 281, 285, 295, 301, 305, 311, 319

Cell phones, p485

Celsius scale, 176, 380, p380, 381

Central Prairies, 92

Change of state, 304

Chapter Review and Test Prep, 30–31, 62–63, 94–95, 132–133, 166–167, 188–189, 214–215, 238–239, 262–263, 294–295, 318–319, 348–349, 382–383, 406–407, 444–445, 470–471, 502–503

Charon, p465

Cheese, p313

Chemical change, 298, p299, 301, p301, 309, p310–311, 310–313 light from, 370 using, p312, 312–313, p313

Chemical energy, 359, 360, 362, 363, p363, c363

Chemical properties, 301, p301

Chemist, 296

Chicago water-cleaning plants, p161

Chimpanzees, 53, p53

Chromium, c204

Chrysalis, 45, p45

Circulatory system, p124

Cirrocumulus clouds, p191

Cirrostratus clouds, p191

Cirrus clouds, p175, p190

Clarinet, p395

Classifying, 30, 132, 238, 244, c244, 262, c262, 406, c406

Clay, 208, p209

Clean air, 120, p121

Cleanliness, 120, p121

Clean water, 120, p120–121, 160, p160

Climate
in Alaskan tundra, c80
in desert, c78
in forest ecosystem, c82
fossil records and, 56
in Kansas grassland, c76
in tropical forest, c84

Clouds, 175, p175, 190–191, p190–191

Coal, 248, c248, p249, 493

Coast, p224

Collecting Data, 26, 27, 128, 129, 185, 211, 234, 258, 378, 379, 388, 414, 466

Color of minerals, 202, c203

Combined force, 334–335, p334–335

Communicating, 143, 271, 324, 356, 415, 511

Communication by whales, p399

Community, p67, 74, 108

Compare and Contrast, 5, 9, 25, 31, 197, 199, 203, 215, c215, 245, c245, 249, 255, 263, c263, 389, 393, 397, 407, 453, 459, 465, 471

Comparing Data, p92, 92–93, p93

Competition, p110, 110–113 cycle of, c113 kinds of, 112–113

Compost, 251, p251

Compression wave, p387, 396

Computer, p475, 484, 485, p489, 495

Computer Engineer, 472

Conclusions. See Draw conclusions

Condensation, p147, 157, p159

Cones (coniferous trees), 16, p17, 24

Coniferous trees, p2, 16–17, 82, p83

Conservation, p243, 250–251, 254, p254

Conservation Career, 264, p264

Constant speed, 330

Constellation, p419, 438, p439

Consumer, p98, 106, 107

Copper, c204, c205

Coral, p89

Core, p218, 223, c223

Coyotes, 74, p74, c75, 104

Crayfish, p106

Crest, 365

Crinoids, p200

Crocoite, c203

Crops
soil for, 251
water for, p153

Cross Curricular Links
Art in Science, 19, 41, 49, 71, 107, 117, 225, 257, 375, 401, 437, 455, 479

Health in Science, 123, 151, 313

Math in Science, p28, 28–29, p29, c29, 43, 55, c60, 60–61, 81, p92, 92–93, p93, 119, c130, 130–131, 157, 164–165, p164–165, p186, 186–187, c187, 207, p212, 212–213, p213, c213, 231, c236, 236–237, 253, 260–261, p260–261, 289, 292–293, p292–293, 316–317, p316–317, 335, 337, 346–347, p346–347, 363, 380–381, p380–381, 399, 433, 442, p442, c443, 457, c468, 468–469, 497, 500–501

Social Studies in Science, 11, 21, 53, 209, 227, 283, 307, 329, 483, 493

Technology in Science, 87, 127, 303, 463, 487

Writing in Science, 13, 15, 17, 23, 31, 39, 47, 57, 63, 75, 79, 82, 85, 89, 95, 103, 111, 115, 120, 125, 133, 155, 161, 167, 175, 183, 189, 201, 204, 215, 223, 233, 239, 247, 251, 263, 279, 287, 295, 309, 319, 327, 333, 339, 349, 359, 367, 369, 371, 373, 383, 391, 395, 407, 425, 431, 439, 445, 461, 471, 481, 485, 489, 503

Crust, p218, 223, c223

Cubic unit, 288, p288

Cumulus clouds, p175, p190

Dam, 492, p493

Data. *See* Collecting Data; Interpreting Data

Daou, Doris, 504

Daphnia, 151, p151

Day
on Earth, 459
on Mars, 459

Day and night, p424, 424–425, p425

Daylight
seasonal hours of, c431

Death stage, c44

Decay, 118, 119, p195, 206

Deciduous
forests, 82, p83
plants, p3, 14

Decomposer, 118, p119

Density, p275, 286, p286, 286–287, p287

Descriptive Writing in Science, 7, 39, 63, 75, 82, 85, 155, 183, 309, 319, 327, 349, 359, 369, 383, 391, 395, 431, 461, 503

Desert, p78, 78–79, p79, 181
climate in, c78
Joshua Tree National Park, p79
wind erosion in, 232

Details. *See* Main idea and details

Development stage, c44

Diagram, c421

Diamond hardness, 203

Dickey, Jean, 240

Digestion, p123, 123
chemical changes in, 312
water for, 151

Dinosaurs, 64
fossils, 56
skulls, p54

Directed Inquiry, Explore, 4, 36, 68, 100, 148, 172, 196, 220, 244, 276, 300, 324, 356, 388, 420, 452, 476

Discovery Videos, 33, 144, 217, 272, 273, 416, 473, 512

Disease, 126

Dissolve, 308, p309

Douglas fir trees, 118, p118

Draw Conclusions, 101, 105, 109, 113, 133, c133, 318

Drinking water, 120, p153

Drought, 115

Dune grass, p73

Dwarf planet, 465, p465

Eagles, 104, 109, p109

Ear, 400, p400

Eardrum, p400

Earth, p424, 424–425, p425, 453, p456, 457, 458, p458
  axis of, 424
  changes from erosion, 232–233
  extremes on, c460, p461
  fossils and, 56
  Hubble Space Telescope and, 446
  layers of, 223–225
  life on, 460–461, p460–461
  lunar eclipse and, 434
  Moon and, 432–433
  plates on, 461
  rotation of, 425, 459
  seasons and, 428–429, p428–429
  shapes on surface of, 224, p224, p225
  size of, 459
  water on, 148, 154, p154

Earthquake, 228, p228
  damage from, 229, p229
  measuring, c236, 236–237

Earthworm, p206

Echo, 399

Eclipse, p419, 434, p434

Ecosystem, 71–75
  desert, p78, 78–79, p79
  forest, 82–83, p83
  freshwater, 86, p86, p87
  grasslands, 76–77, p77
  groups within, 74, p75
  parts of, 72, c72
  saltwater, 88, p89
  tropical forest, 84, p85
  tundra, p80, 80–81, p81
  water, 86–89

Egg
  animal growth and, 44
  butterfly, p44
  frog, p46

Electrical energy, 359, c363, 367, p374, 374–377, p375, p376, c377

Electrical Engineer, 384

Electric charge, p354–355, 374–375

Electric circuit, p355, p376, 376–377, c377

Electric current, p355, 376, p376, 376–377, c377

Electricity, p370
  form changed by, c377
  in home, 480, p480
  light from, 371
  past and present technology and, 482
  producing, p492, 492–493, p493
  in space missions, 384
  water for, 152, p153

Element, p274, 282, p282, 283, p283

Energy, 354, 357, p357, 359, p359
  changing form by, 362–363
  electrical, p374, 374–377, p375, p376, c377
  from food, 123
  in food web, 108
  forms of, c363
  from fuels, 248
  future sources of, 494–495, p494–495
  heat, p366, 366–369, p367, p368, p369
  light, 370–373
  for living things, 106–109
  of motion, 361
  for new and recycled goods, p255
  sound and, 386, 398

  sources of, 490
  technology and, 490–495
  travel of, 364–365, p364–365
  in waves, 365

Environment, 71
  of California redwood tree, p73
  change in, 114–117
  clean, p121
  healthy for people, 120–123
  living things return to, 116
  patterns of change in, 118–119

Epedocles, p283

Equator, 429

Erosion, p219, 232–233, p233, 234–235

Eruption, 221, p221

Estimating and Measuring, 172, 210, 211, 269, 290, 291, 414, 452

Evaporation, p146, 157, 158, p159, 309, 369

Everglades, 86, p86

Evergreen trees. See Coniferous trees

Exercise, p124, 124–125

Exercising in Space, 350–351, p350–351

Exhaust, 179

Experiment. See Full Inquiry, Experiment

Experimenting. See Investigating and Experimenting

Explore. See Directed Inquiry, Explore

Expository Writing in Science, 13, 17, 23, 31, 47, 57, 79, 95, 111, 133, 161, 189, 201, 204, 223, 233, 247, 251, 279, 287, 295, 339, 367, 425, 445, 481, 485, 489

Extinct, p3, 23, 55

Fahrenheit scale, 176, 380, p380, 381

Fall, 430

Farm water, p153

Ferrets, 108, 109, p109

Ferris wheel, 342, p342

Fiber optic technology, 485, p485

Filtration of water, p160, 161, p250

Fire, 311
environmental change from, 117, p117
impact on ecosystem, p75

Firefighter, 320

Fish, p41, p102
helping one another, 105
school of, p102
swimming speeds of, c60, 60–61

Flooding, 115, p115, p183

Florida water, p250

Flowering plants, p14, 14–15, p24

Flowers
bees and, p104
in first plants, 24

Fluorite, c205

Flu virus, p126

Food
adaptation for gathering, 49, p49
animals and, 7, 39, 74
digestion of, p123, 123
energy from, 123
handling of, 122
health and, c130, 130–131
healthful, 122
in leaves, 8
minerals in, 204
mold on, 90–91, p90–91
plants and, 7
sources of, p121
storage of, 122
variety of, 122
water for, p153

Food chain, 108

Food web
changes in, 109
energy in, 108

Force, p323, 332, p332, p333, p338
combined, 334–335, p334–335
motion and, 332

Forest, p118

Forest ecosystems, 82–83, p83
climate in, c82
tropical forests, 84, c84, p85

Forming Questions and Hypotheses, 140, 268, 412, 508

Fossil, 22, p54, 54–57, p55, p56
as fuel, 360
plant, p3, 22, 23–25, p23, p24
in sedimentary rock, 200, p200

Freezing water, 156, p157, 231, 311

Freshwater, 155, p155, 258–259

Freshwater ecosystems, 86, p86, p87

Freshwater resources, 258–259, p258–259

Friction, p323, 333

Frog life cycle, 46, p47

Fruit
seeds in, p21

Fuel, 248, 360
burning, p370
for generating electricity, 493
renewable, 361

Full Inquiry, Experiment, 140–143, 268–271, 412–415, 508–511

Galena, c205

Galileo, 496, p496

Garbage
recycling, 256
removal, 120
See also Trash

Gas, 281, p281, p305
air as, 398
in atmosphere, 176
exhaust, 179
explosion of, p308
in leaves, p8, 8, p9
liquid as, 369
mass of, 284
water as, 157

Gas giants (outer planets), 462

Generators, 492, p492, 493

Germ, 126
avoiding, p126, 126–127, p127
in water, 160–161

Germinate, 2, p2, 3, 20, p21, 26–27, 28–29

Glacier, p224, 231, p231

Glass
recycled, p254–255, 254–255

Global Positioning System (GPS), 484

Gneiss, p201

Gold, 203

Golden eagle, 104, 109

GPS. See Global Positioning System (GPS)

Gram, 284

Granite, p201, c205

Graphic Organizer, c5, c31, c37, c63, c95, c101, c133, c149, c167, c173, c189, c197, c215, c221, 229, c239, c245, c263, c277, c301, c319, c325, c349, c357, c383, c389, c407, c453, c477, c502

Grass, p11, 76

Grassland, 76–77, p77
climate in, c76
comparing data about, p92, 92–93, p93

Grass seeds, 68

Gravity, p322, 336, p336, 336–337, 361, 460
in space, 350–351, p350–351

Great Barrier Reef, p89

Great Plains food web, 108, p108

Great Red Spot (Jupiter), p462

Green plants, 106

Ground squirrels, 74, c75

Groundwater, p146, 155, p158–159

Groupings of animals, 39–43

Groups
in ecosystems, 74, c75
living in, 104

Grow best, 68

Growth stage, c44

Guided Inquiry, Investigate, 26–27, 58–59, 90–91, 128–129, 162–163, 184–185, 210–211, 234–235, 258–259, 290–291, 314–315, 344–345, 378–379, 402–403, 440–441, 466–467, 498–499

Habitats, 72

Hail, 159

Halite, c205

Hand lens, 289, p289

Hardness of minerals, 203, c203

Hawaiian volcano, p227

Health
avoiding germs and, p126, 126–127, p127
foods and, c130, 130–131
maintaining, 124–127
minerals and, 204, c205

Health in Science, 123, 151, 313

Hearing, 400, p400

Heart, 124, p124

Heat, c377
from burning, p370
from electrical heaters, c377

Heat energy, p366, 366–369, p367, p368, p369
matter and, 368
sources of, 367, p367
thermal energy as, 366

Heating and cooling, 480
from solar energy, 494, p494

Hematite, 248, p249

Hemlocks, 118–119

Herbivore, p98, 106, p107

Hexagon, 164

Hibernate, p34, 52, p52

Highways, p486
technology for, 487
tools for building, 487, p487

Hill, p225, p232

Homes
habitats as, 72
technology in, c480, 480–481, p480–481, p482, 482–483, p483

Hoover Dam, p493

Horizon, p425

Horne, Clifton, 408

Housing, p121, 251
See also Shelter

Howard, Ayanna, 472

How to Read Science, xx, xxi, 5, 37, 101, 149, 173, 197, 221, 245, 277, 301, 325, 357, 389, 421, 453, 477;
See also Target Reading Skills

Hubble Space Telescope, p446, 446–447, p447, 463

Humidity, 177

Humus, 209

Hunting by animals, p53

Hurricane, 115, *p*170, 182, *p*183

Hydroelectric power, 492, *p*492, *p*493

Hyena, 111, *p*111

Hygrometer, 177, *p*177

Hypotheses, Forming Questions and, 140, 268, 412, 508

Ice, 155, *p*155, 305, *p*305, 311
heating of, 368, *p*368, 369

Identifying and controlling variables, 140, 268, 508

Igneous rock, *p*194, 200, 201, *p*201
copper in, *c*205
volcanoes and, *p*227

Illness, 126

Imprint, 58–59

Inclined plane, 340, *p*340

Indianapolis weather, *p*186, 186–187, *c*187

Inferences. *See* Make Inferences

Inferring, 30, 59, 62, 94, 100, 128, 129, 148, 162, 163, 166, 172, 188, 196, 215, 239, 259, 262, 276, 294, 300, 318, 345, 348, 382, 402, 403, 406, 407, 441, 444, 467, 499, 502

Information processing technology, 485

Infrared telescopes, 504

Inherited, *p*34, 48

Inner ear, *p*400

Inner planets, 458–459

Insects, *c*42, *p*83
ancient, 55, *p*55
in grasslands, *p*77
in tropical forests, *p*84

Instincts, 52, *p*52

Instruments, 389, *p*392, 393, *p*393, *p*394, 394–395, *p*395

Interaction of living things, *c*103, 103–105

Internet, 26, 36, 58, 68, 87, 90, 100, 128, 148, 162, 164, 172, 184, 186, 196, 199, 210, 212, 220, 234, 244, 258, 260, 276, 290, 292, 300, 303, 314, 324, 346, 356, 388, 420, 442, 447, 452, 476, 487

Interpreting Data, 26, 27, 90, 91, 94, 133, 184, 185, 235, 291, 415

Intestines, *p*122, 123

Invention, *p*474, 479

Invertebrates, 42, *p*43

Investigate. *See* Guided Inquiry, Investigate

Investigating and Experimenting, 268, 412, 508

Iron, *c*204, *c*205, 248, *c*248, *p*249
in foods, 204
rusting of, 311

Islands
erosion and, 232, *p*232

Joshua Tree National Park, *p*79

Journal. *See* Science Journal

Jupiter, 457, 462

Keck telescope, *p*436

Kilogram, 284

Kilometer, 288

Kinetic energy, *p*354, 361, *p*361, 363, *c*363, *p*363

Konza Prairie, Kansas, *p*77

Lab Zone, 4, 26–27, 29, 32, 36, 58–59, 61, 64, 68, 90–91, 93, 96, 100, 128–129, 131, 135, 136, 140–143, 148, 162–163,165, 168, 172, 184–185, 187, 191, 192, 196, 210–211, 213, 216, 220, 234–235, 237, 240, 244, 258–259, 261, 264, 268–271, 276, 290–291, 293, 296, 300, 314–315, 317, 320, 324, 344–345, 347, 351, 352, 356, 378–379, 381, 384, 388, 402–403, 405, 408, 412–415, 420, 440–441, 443, 447, 448, 452, 466–467, 469, 472, 476, 498–499, 501, 504, 508–511; *See also* Activities

Lakes, 86, p224

Land
on Earth, p155
for trash, 252

Landfill, p252, 252–253

Landform, p218, 224, 232–233

Land resources, 251

Landslides, 229

Large intestine, 122, 123

Larva, p35, 37, p44, 45, p45

Lava, p218, 226, p226, p227

Lawn sprinklers, p490, 491

Layers of Earth, 223–225

Lead, c205

Leaf veins, 9, p9

Leaves, p8, 8–9, p9

Length measurement, 288

Leppershey, Hans, 496

Lever, 341, p341

Levine, Elissa R., 216, p216

Lichen, p81, 82

Life. See Living things

Life cycle, 44–47
of butterfly, 45
of frog, 46, p46
mammal, 46, p47
of plant, p21
of sea jelly, c37
stages, c44
vertebrate, 46

Light, c363, c377
from burning, p370
on Moon, 433
path of, 371
reflecting of, 372, p372
refracting of, 372–373, p373
shadows and, p426, 426–427, p427
speed of, p398
from Sun, 461
travel of, 372–373

Light and dark patterns, 423

Light energy, c363, 370–373

Lightning, 117, p374

Limestone, p202

Line of symmetry, 164

Lion, 111, p111

Liquid, 280, p280, 284, p292, 305, p305

Little Bear, 438

Little bones in eardrum, p400

Little Dipper, 438, p439

Living/growing space, 7

Living things
competition among, 110–113
on Earth, 460–461
energy for, 106–109
environment for, 71
erosion caused by, 233
helping another living thing, 104
helping one another, 105
interaction of, c103, 103–105
in ocean, c88
patterns of change and, 118–119
return after environmental change, 116
water and, 151, 152
weathering by, 230

Lizard, p56

Loam, p195, c208, 209

Log, p247

Lumber, p246, p247

Lunar eclipse, p419, 434, p434

Lungs, 125, p125

Luster of minerals, 202, c203

Machines
simple, p340, 340–343, p342, p343
work and, 338–339

Magma, p218, 226, p227

Magnetic, 337

Magnetic force, c377

Magnetism, p202, 307, p323, 337, p337

Magnetite, p202

Magnification, 289, p289

Magnolias, p24, p25

Main Idea and Details, 69, 73, 77, 95, 357, 361, 365, 377, 383

Make Inferences, 173, 177, 179, 181, 189

Making and Using Models, 36, 196, 215, 220, 235, 238, 258, 440, 452, 466, 471, 498, 499, 508

Making Operational Definitions, 68

Mammals, p41, 47
See also Animals

Manatees, p86

Mantle, p218, 223, c223

Map, p233, 328, p328

Mars, p456, 457, 458, p458, 459

Marsh water, p156

Mass, p275, 284, c284, 316, p333

Math in Science, 28–29, 43, 55, 60–61, 81, 92–93, 130–131, 157, 164–165, 186–187, 207, 212–213, 231, 236–237, 253, 260–261, 289, 292–293, 316–317, 337, 335, 346–347, 363, 380–381, 399, 404–405, 433, 442, 457, 468–469, 497, 500–501

Matter, p274, 279, p279
  change in, 300
  chemical changes in, 299, p310–311, 310–313
  combining, p306, 306–309
  describing, 279–283
  forms of, 280–281
  heat and, 368
  measuring properties of, 284–289
  parts of, 282–283
  physical changes in, 298, 303–305
  properties of, 274, 290–291
  sound and, 398
  speed and, 332
  state of, 304
  temperature of, 304

Maturation of tomato plant, 29

Measurement
  of Earthquake, c236, 236–237
  of mass, 284, p284
  of properties of matter, 284–289, p290, 290–291, p292–293
  of speed of wind, 172

of temperature, 380–381, p380–381
of volume, 285, p285

Measuring. See Estimating and Measuring

Meat-eating animal, p48

Mechanical energy, 359

Melting, 368, p368, 369

Mercury, p456, 457, 458, p458

Metals, 248

Metamorphic rock, p194, 201, p201

Meter, 288

Metric system
  rules and tapes for measuring, 288, 289
  units for mass, 284

Mica, c203

Microscope, p126

Microwave, 488, p488

Migrate, p34, 52, p52

Millimeters, 292

Mimicry, 50, p51

Mineral, p195, 199
  identifying, 202
  properties of, c203
  using, 204, c204, c205
  water and, 230

Mississippi River flooding, p115

Mixture, p298, 306–307, p306–307, 316–317, p316–317
  separating, p314, 314–315, c315

Models. See Making and Using Models

Mold, 54, p54, p90, 90–91, c91, p91

Mold on food, 90–91, p90–91

Mollusks, c42, p43

Molybdenite, c203

Monkey sounds, p401

Moon (Earth), 432–435, 459
  distance from Earth, 433
  phases of, 434, p435
  revolution of, 432–433
  rotation of, 432, 433
  shape of, p432, 432–433, p433, 434–435, p435
  Sun and, 434

Moon landing, 497, p497

Moons, c470
  of Jupiter, 462
  of Mars, 459
  of Mercury, 458
  of Neptune, 464
  of Pluto, 465, p465
  of Saturn, 463
  of Uranus, 464
  of Venus, 453, 458
  See also Moon (Earth)

Moon trees, 134–135

Moose, p83

Mosses, 82

Moth, 105, p105

Motion, p322, 325, p325, 327, p327
  energy of, 361
  force and, 332–337, p334–335

Mountain, p225

Mount Palomar Observatory, 496, p496

Mt. St. Helens environmental change, 116

Mountain
  forming of, 220

Mouth, 123

Museum Display Card, 37

Mushrooms, p119

Music, 391

Narrative Writing in Science, 15, 89, 103, 175, 239, 263, 333, 371, 373, 407, 439

NASA (National Aeronautics and Space Administration)
Astronomers, 504
Chemist, 296
Computer Engineer, 472
Jean Dickey, 240
Electrical Engineer, 384
Electricity in Space
Exercising in Space, 350–351, p350–351
Clifton Horne, 408
Hubble Space Telescope, p446, 446–447, p447
Elissa R. Levine, 216, p216
Plant Researcher, 32
Stuart Roosa and Moon trees, 134–135
Eric Stolen, 96
Studying Clouds from Space, 190–191, p190–191
Teachers, 504

National Highway System, 486, p486

Natural events
environmental change through, 115, p115

Natural gas, 248, 493

Natural resource, p242, 247
endless supply of, 249
landfills and, p252, 252–253
limited nature of, 248–249

Navigation tools, 484

Needles on plants, p9

Needs of people, 120–121

Negative charge, 374–375

Neptune, 457, p457, 464, p465
Night. *See* Day and night

Nonrenewable resource, p242, 248

Noon, p425

North Pole, 424, p424

North Star, 439

Nutrients, 122, p195, 206, p251

Oakland earthquake, p228

Oak leaf, p9

Oboe, 395

Observing, 4, 27, 58, 59, 68, 90, 100, 140, 163, 172, 211, 234, 258, 259, 268, 276, 300, 324, 344, 345, 356, 378, 379, 388, 402, 403, 420, 441, 476

Ocean, p224
life in, c88
saltwater ecosystem in, 88, p89

Oceanographer, 168

Oil, 248, c248
burning for electric power, 493
pumping, p248

Omnivore, 106, p107

Operational Definition. *See* Making Operational Definitions

Optical fibers, 485, p485

Orbit, p450, 456
of Earth, p428–429
of Moon, p432
of Neptune, 464
of Pluto, 465
See also Revolution

Ore, c205, 248, c248
iron in, c205
sources of, 249

Orion constellation, 438

Outer ear, p400

Outer planets, 462–465, c468

Oxygen, 8, p9
competition for, 112
in plants, p9

Ozone, 179

Palm viper, p85

Paper, p246, 260, c260–261

Parachutes on seeds, p19

Park Ranger, 136

Parts of matter, 282–283

Patterns
light and dark, 423
repeating, 428–429
sequence of, c421
star, 438–439
in tables, c468,
468–469
See also Moon (Earth);
Moons

Pecan tree leaf, p9

Pelican adaptation, p49

People
healthy environment for,
120–123
needs of, 120–121

Percussion instruments,
p392, 393, p393

Periodic table, p275,
283, p283

**Persuasive Writing in
Science,** 120, 125,
167, 215, 471

Petals, p15

Petrified fossil, 22,
p22, 23, p23

Phase, p419, 434, p435

Phosphorus, 204, c204

Physical change, 298,
p298, p303, 303–305,
p304

Pillbugs, 100, 111

Pine cones, 16, p17, 19

Pitch, p386, 392, p392,
p393, 394

Plain, p225

Planet, p450, 456, c470
dwarf, 465, p465
Hubble Space Telescope
and, 446
inner, 457, 458–459
outer, 457, 462–465
Venus and Earth as, 453
Planetoids, 465

Plant, 2
animal interaction with,
p98–p99, 106, p106–
107
changes over time, 24,
p24–25
compared with animals, 5
desert, 78
environmental change
and, 114–117
in Everglades, 86, p86
flowering, p14, 14–15
in forest ecosystems, 82,
p83
fossils, 22–25, 56
germination time for,
28–29
in grasslands, 76, p77
grouping of, 14–17
growth of, 18–21
life cycle of, p21
parts of, 2, 7–9, 10,
11, 12
in saltwater ecosystems,
88, p89
soil for best growth, 68
in tropical forest,
84, p84
in tundra, 80, p81
weathering by,
230, p230

Plant-eating animal,
p48

Plant Researcher, 32

Plants
alike and different, 4

Plateau, p224

Plates on Earth, 461

Pluto, p456, 457, 465

Poison, p51

Pollen, p15, p17

Pollen cones, 16

Pollinate, p2, 15

Polluted water, 149

Pollution
alerts for, 179
from burning fuel, 493
from electric power
production, 492, 493

Polyp, 37

Population, 67, 74, p74,
c75

Porcupine, 50, p50

Position, p322, 327,
328, p328
on map, 328
potential energy and,
360

Positive charge,
374–375

Potassium, c204

Potential energy, p354,
360, p360, 361, p361

Prairie, p77
comparing grasslands
and, p92, 92–93, p93
energy in food web of,
108, p108

Prairie dogs, 104, 108,
109

Precipitation, p147, 158,
p158–159, 159, 180

Predator, 107, 111,
128–129

Predicting, 62, 94, 133,
162, 166, 188, 215,
269, 276, 294, 314,
315, 318, 344, 345,
348, 382, 406, 412,
420, 440, 471, 476,
502

Pressure, p274, 281

Prey, 107, 111, p111

Process Skills. *See*
Science Process Skills

Producer, p98, 106,
p106

Property, p274, 276, 279
light and, p372
measuring, 284–289

Protection and animal adaptation, 50, p50, p51

Pulley, 343, p343

Pulling forces, 334–335

Pupa, p35, 45, p45

Purification of water, p120

Purple loosestrife, 112, p112

Pushing, p338

Quartz, 202

Questioning. See Forming Questions and Hypotheses

Quiz Show, 30, 62, 94, 132, 166, 188, 214, 238, 262, 294, 318, 348, 382, 406, 444, 470, 502

Raccoon, p107

Radio waves, 437

Rain, 150, p158, 159, 175, 180, p181, p183
in deserts, 181
erosion from, 232–233

Rainbow lorikeets, p84

Rain gauge, 177, p177

Rainwater, 251

Rattlesnake, p78

Reading Skills. See Target Reading Skills

Recycle, p243, 250, 254, p254, 257, 264
energy for, p255
glass, p254, 255, 261
using recycled materials, 256, p256

Recycling Plant Worker, 264, p264

"Red Planet" (Mars), 459, p459

Reducing resource uses, 257

Redwood tree, p73

Reflect, p354, 372, p372

Refract, p355, 372–373, p373

Relative position, p322, 329, p329

Renewable energy source, 361

Renewable resource, p242, 247, p247, 491

Reproduction stage, c44

Reptile, p41

Reservoir, p121

Resource
classifying, 244
competition for, 110, p110
conserving, 250–251
forests and, p246
freshwater, 258–259, p258–259
land, 251
natural, p242, 247
nonrenewable, p242
protecting, 250–253
renewable, p242, 247
reusing, 254–257
rock as, p194
three Rs of, 257
uses of, c248

Respiratory system, 125, p125

Reuse, 257

Revolution, p418, 428
of Earth, 428–429, p428–429, 459
of inner planets, 458
of Jupiter, 462
of Moon, 432, 433
time for, 468, c468
of Uranus, 464
See also Orbit

Richter scale, 236

Rings
of Jupiter, 462
of Neptune, 464
of Saturn, p463
of Uranus, 464, p464

River, 155, p155, p225
ecosystems in, 86
oceans and, 88
transportation on, 487

Roads. See Highways

Rock, 199, p199
breaking through weather and erosion, p230, 230–233
formation of, 199–201
layers, 196
as resource, p194
sizes of pieces, c231
in soil, 208, 212
under soil, p207

Rock Collectors, 197

Rock groups, 200

Roman engineering, 478, p478, 479, p479, 496, p496

Roosa, Stuart, 134–135

Root, 10, p10, 11
edible, p11
of grassland plant, 76, p77
of tundra plant, 80

Root hair, 11

Rotation, p418, 424, p425, 428
of Earth, 425, 458, 459
of inner planets, 458
of Jupiter, 462
of Moon, 432, 433
of Neptune, 464
of Pluto, 465
of Uranus, 464

Rust, 311, p311

Saber tooth tiger, 55

Saguaro cactus, 181, p181

Salt, c205, 499, 508

Saltwater ecosystems, 88, p89

Sand in soil, 208, p208

Satellites, 484, p484, 496, p496

Saturn, 457, p457, 463, p463

Saxophone, p395

Science Fair Projects, 144, 272, 416, 512

Science Journal, 7, 13, 15, 17, 23, 39, 47, 57, 75, 82, 85, 89, 96, 103, 111, 115, 120, 161, 175, 183, 201, 204, 223, 233, 251, 279, 287, 309, 327, 333, 339, 359, 367, 369, 371, 373, 391, 385, 425, 431, 439, 461, 479, 481, 485, 489

Science Process Skills,
Classifying, 30, 132, 238, 244, 262, 406, 378, 379, 388, 414, 466

Collecting Data, 26, 27, 128, 129, 185, 211, 234, 258, 378, 379, 388, 414, 466

Communicating, 143, 271, 324, 356, 415, 511

Estimating and Measuring, 172, 210, 211, 269, 290, 291, 324, 356, 414, 415, 452, 511

Forming Questions and Hypotheses, 140, 268, 412, 508

Identifying and Controlling Variables, 140, 268, 508

Inferring, 30, 59, 62, 94, 100, 128, 129, 148, 162, 163, 166, 172, 188, 196, 215, 239, 259, 262, 276, 294, 300, 318, 345, 348, 382, 402, 403, 406, 407, 441, 444, 467, 499, 502

Interpreting Data, 26, 27, 90, 91, 94, 133, 184, 185, 235, 291,

Investigating and Experimenting, 268, 412, 508

Making and Using Models, 36, 196, 215, 220, 235, 238, 258, 440, 452, 466, 471, 498, 499, 508

Making Operational Definitions, 68

Observing, 4, 27, 58, 59, 68, 90, 100, 140, 163, 172, 211, 234, 258, 259, 268, 276, 300, 324, 344, 345, 356, 378, 379, 388, 402, 403, 420, 441, 476

Predicting, 62, 94, 133, 162, 166, 188, 215, 269, 276, 294, 314, 315, 318, 344, 345, 348, 382, 406, 412, 420

Scientific Methods for Experimenting, xxvi

Screw, 341, p341

Seagulls, p112

Sea jelly, 37, c42, p43

Seasons, p181, 428–429, 430, c431, p431
in Sonoran Desert, 181
start patterns and, 439

Seattle weather, p186, 186–187, c187

Sedimentary rock, p194, 200, 201, p201

Seed
in coniferous plant, 16, p17
in flowering plant, 15
germinating and growing, 20, 26–27
how do different kinds of seeds germinate?, 26–27, c27
making of, 15
parts of, p20
in pine cones, 19
releasing, 19
scattering, p18, 18–19

Seed cone, 16

Seed leaf, 2, p2, 20

Seedling, p3, 20, p21

Sequence, 37, 45, 51, 63, 221, 225, 229, c239, 239, 421, 423, 427, 429, 435, 445, 477, 491, 495, 503

Signal Words, 63

Sereno, Paul, 64

Shadows, p426, 426–427, p427

Shale, p201

Shapes on Earth's surface, 224, p224, p225

Sheep as herbivore, p107

Shelter, 39, 120, p121

Shipping of food, p121

Shooting star, p176

Shrews, 101

Sidewinder rattlesnake, p78

Silt in soil, 208, p208

Simple machines, p340, 340–343, p342, p343

Size measurement, 288

Skunks, 50

Slate, p201

Sleet, 159

Small intestine, 123, p123

Smell of mineral, 203

Smog, 179, p179

Snow, p150, 159, 180

Social Studies in Science, 11, 21, 53, 209, 227, 283, 307, 329, 483, 493

Sodium, 204, c204

Soil, 71, 194, p195, 206, 251
animals in, 212, p212, c213, p213
comparing, 208, p208
conserving, 251
in environment, 71
growing grass seeds in, 68
ingredients in, 209
layers of, p207
parts of, 206
water in, 210–211
weathering of, 230

Soil Scientist, 216

Solar energy, 494, p494

Solar system, p450, 456, p456
inner planets in, 458–459
life in, 460–461
movement of objects in, 456–457
outer planets in, 462–465
parts of, 455–457

Solid, 280, p280, 305, p305
mass of, 284
sound waves in, 398, 399
speed of sound through, c404, 404–405, c405
water as, 368, p368, 369

Solid rock, p207

Solution, p298, 308, p308, 309, p309

Sonoran Desert, 181

Sound, c363, c377, 386
causes of, 391, 392–393
comparing speeds of, c404, 404–405, c405
in industry, 408
matter and, 398, 399
speed of, p398, c399
using air to make sound, 394–395

Sound waves, p396, 396–397, p397
echoes and, 399
hearing with ear, 400, p400

South Dakota Badlands, 56, p57

South Pole, 424, p424

Space, 112

Space (outer), 350–351, p350–351

Space shuttle, p176

Speed, p322, 330, p330, 332
constant, 330
relating to distance and time, 346–347, p346–347
variable, 331

Speed of light, p398

Speed of sound, p398, c399, c404, 404–405, c405

Spencer, Percy, p488

Spring (season), 430

Spring water in Florida, 86, p87, p155

Sputnik 1, 496, p496

Star, p418, 423
in constellations, 438, p438
Hubble Space Telescope and, 446
movement of, 439
patterns of, 436–439
Sun as, 423
telescope and, 436–437

Star tracks, p439

State of Matter, 304

Steam, 368

Steel, c205, 248

Stem, 10, 12, p12, 12–13, p13

Stinkbugs, p84

Stolen, Eric, 96

Stomach, 123, p123

Storms, p182, 182–183

Stratocumulus clouds, p191

Stratus clouds, p190

Streak mark on mineral, 202, c203

Stream, 86

Strep throat, p127

Stutte, Gary, 32

Subsoil, p207

Sugar in leaves, p8

Summarize, 325, 331, 341, 343, 349

Summer, 80, p428, 430

Sun, p424, 424–425, p425
day and night and, p424
energy from, 359, 461
light and dark patterns and, 423
light from, 370
lunar eclipse and, 434
Moon and, 433, 434
planet's revolution and, 468
in plants, p9
pollution and, 179
seasons and, 428–429, p428–429, 430
shadows and, p426, 426–427, p427
solar energy from, 494
in solar system, 455

Sunlight, 8, 9

Sunrise times, 442, p442, c443

Sunset times, 442, p442, c443

Swimming speeds of fish, c60, 60–61

Symmetrical, 164

System, p2, 8

Tables, 212, 236

Tadpole, p47

Take-Home Activity, 29, 32, 61, 64, 93, 96, 131, 135, 136, 165, 168, 187, 191, 192, 213, 216, 237, 240, 261, 264, 293, 296, 317, 320, 347, 351, 352, 381, 384, 405, 408, 443, 447, 448, 469, 472, 501, 504

Talc, 203

Taproot, 10

Target Reading Skills
Cause and Effect, 149, 152, 159, 167, 277, 281, 285, 295, 301, 305, 311, 319

Compare and Contrast, 5, 9, 25, 31, 197, 199, 203, 215, 245, 249, 255, 263, 389, 393, 397, 407, 453, 459, 465, 471

Draw Conclusions, 101, 105, 109, 113, 133, 318

Main Idea and Details, 69, 73, 77, 95, 357, 361, 377, 383

Make Inferences, 173, 177, 179, 181, 189

Sequence, 37, 45, 51, 63, 221, 225, 229, 239, 421, 423, 427, 429, 435, 445, 477, 491, 495

Summarize, 325, 331, 341, 343, 349

Tar pit fossils, 55

Taste of mineral, 203

Teachers, 504

Technology, p474, 479
bridges and, 478
energy sources and, 490–495
in home, c480, 480–481, p480–481
past and present, p482, 482–483, p483
timeline for, 496, p496–497
transportation, c501
types of new, 484–489
unexpected uses of, 488–489

Technology in Science, 87, 303, 463, 487; See also Internet

Telephone, 497, p497

Telescope, p419, 436, p436, 436–437, 496, p496
Galileo and, 448
Hubble Space Telescope, p446, 446–447, p447, 463
infrared, 504

Temperature, c188
comparing, p186, 186–187, c187
of matter, 304
measuring, 176, 380–381, p380–381
seasons and, 430
of Sun, 455
water and, 151

Test Prep. See Chapter Review and Test Prep

Test Talk, 137, 265, 409, 505

Thaller, Michelle, 504

Thawing, 231

Thermal energy, p355, c363, 366

Thermometer, p380

Time, distance, and speed, 346–347, p346–347

Timeline for technology, 496, p496–497

Tool, p474, 479
for extending our senses, 484
for information processing, 484
for transporting materials, 486–487

Topsoil, p206, p207

Tornado, p170, 182, p182, p183

Touch to identify mineral, 203

Trait, p35, 40

Transportation
technology and, 486–487, c501
water for, 152

Trash, 252, c252, p252, 253

Trees, 14
competition among, p110
coniferous, 16–17
in forest ecosystems, 82–83, p83
growth of, p118
as renewable resources, 247
in tundra, p81

Trilobites, p200

Tropical forest ecosystem, 84, p85

Trough, 365

Trumpet, 394, p394

Tundra, 67, p80, c80, 80–81, p81

Tyrannosaurus rex (T. rex), 56, p56

Uranus, 457, p457, 464, p464

Ursa Minor, p489

Valley, 224, p224

Variables. *See* Identifying and controlling variables

Variable speed, 331, p331

Veins in leaves, p9

Venus, 453, p456, 457, 458, p458, 459

Vertebrate, p34, 40, p41

Vibration, p386, 392, p393, 394, p396

Vipers, p85

Virus, p126

Vocal cords, 394, p394

Volcano, p225
environmental change from, 116
eruption of, 221, p221, p222, p227
formation of, 226, p227
igneous rock from, p200

Volume, p275, p284, 285, p288, p292

Wachee Spring, p87

Washington State winter, p180

Waste
removal of, 120
water and, 151

Water
in air, 177
change from liquid to solid, 305, p305
cleaning of, 160–161, p161
in clouds, 175
competition for, p110
conserving, 250
creatures in, 151
on Earth, 154, p154
ecosystems in, 86–89
in environment, 71
erosion by, 232, p232, 233
filtering, p250
forms of, p156, 156–161, p157, p158–159, p160–161
fresh, 155, p155
importance of, 151–155
for industry, p153
in leaves, p8, 9
plant and animal needs for, 7
in plants, 10
protecting, p250
purification of, p120
rain and, 150
in roots, 11
seeds scattered by, p18
in soil, 210–211
sound waves in, 398, p399
sources of, p121
in stem, 12
uses of, 152, c153
waves in, 364
weathering and, 230, 231

Water cycle, *p*146, 158, 162–163

Water ecosystems, 86–89

Water pollution, 149

Water vapor, *p*146, 154, *p*159, 180, *p*305, 368

Water wheel, *p*490

Wave
compression, *p*387, 396
energy as, *p*364
erosion by, *p*232, 233
parts of, 365, *p*365
sound, *p*396, 396–397, *p*397
of sunlight, 370
telescopes and, 437

Weasel, 50

Weather, *p*170–171, 175
changes in, 174
measuring, *p*176, 176–177, *p*177
parts of, 175
patterns of, 180
technology for predicting, 484
weather report and, 173

Weathering, *p*219, 230–233, *c*231

Weather map, 178, *p*178

Weather satellites, 178

Wedge, 340, *p*340

Weeki Wachee River, *p*87

Weight, 284

Wells, *p*121

Western hemlocks, 118–119

Wetland, 67, 86, *p*146, 155, 250, *p*250

Whale
barnacles on, 104
communication by, *p*399

Wheel, 496, *p*496

Wheel and Axle, 342, *p*342

Wind, 177
environmental change from, *p*115
erosion through, 232
measuring speed of, 172
seeds scattered by, *p*18

Wind energy, 491, *p*491, 495

Wind instrument, *p*394, 394–395, *p*395

Windmills, 491, *p*491, 495, *p*495

Windpipe, *p*125

Wind vane, 177, *p*177

Winter, *p*428, 430
in tundra, 80
in Washington State, *p*180

Wolf, 38, *p*38, *p*81, *p*107

Woolly monkeys, *p*84

Word web, *c*69

Work, *p*323, 338–339

Worm, *c*42, *p*43

Wright Brothers, 352, *p*352, 477, 497, *p*497

Writing in Science
Descriptive, 7, 39, 63, 75, 82, 85, 115, 155, 183, 309, 319, 327, 349, 359, 369, 383, 391, 395, 431, 461, 503

Expository, 13, 17, 23, 31, 47, 57, 79, 95, 111, 133, 161, 189, 201, 204, 223, 233, 247, 251, 279, 287, 295, 339, 367, 425, 445, 481, 485, 489

Narrative, 15, 82, 89, 103, 175, 239, 263, 333, 371, 373, 407, 439

Persuasive, 120, 125, 167, 215, 471

Year
on Earth, 459
on Mars, 459

You Are There!, 6, 38, 70, 102, 150, 174, 198, 222, 246, 278, 302, 326, 358, 390, 422, 454, 478

Yucca moth, 105, *p*105

Yucca plant, *p*78

Zebra, *p*401

Credits

Photographs

Every effort has been made to secure permission and provide appropriate credit for photographic material. The publisher deeply regrets any omission and pledges to correct errors called to its attention in subsequent editions.

Unless otherwise acknowledged, all photographs are the property of Scott Foresman, a division of Pearson Education.

Photo locators denoted as follows: Top (T), Center (C), Bottom (B), Left (L), Right (R), Background (Bkgd).

Cover: ©Flip Nicklin/Minden Pictures, ©David Nardini/Getty Images.

Front Matter: iii Daniel J. Cox/Natural Exposures, (T) Getty Images; v ©Frans Lanting/Minden Pictures; vi ©DK Images; vii (R) ©Randy M. Ury/Corbis, (L) ©Breck P. Kent/Animals Animals/Earth Scenes; viii ©Jack Dykinga/Getty Images; xi ©Douglas Peebles/Corbis; xii ©Lloyd Cluff/Corbis; xv ©RNT Productions/Corbis; xxii ©Timothy O'Keefe/Index Stock Imagery; xxiii Getty Images; xxiv (Bkgd) ©Steve Bloom/Getty Images, (C) ©Robert Sullivan/AFP/Getty Images; xxix Getty Images; xxv ©Frank Greenaway/DK Images; xxviii (BL) Getty Images, (CL) ©Dave King/DK Images; xxx ©Comstock Inc.

Unit Dividers: Unit A (Bkgd) Getty Images, (CC) Digital Vision; Unit B (Bkgd) ©Kim Heacox/Getty Images, (BC) Getty Images; Unit C (Bkgd) ©Lester Lefkowitz/Getty Images; Unit D (Bkgd) Corbis

Chapter 1: 1 (B) ©Wolfgang Kaehler/Corbis, (T, C) Getty Images; 2 (T) ©John Warden/Index Stock Imagery, (BL) ©DK Images, (BL) Getty Images, (BR) ©Nigel Cattlin/Photo Researchers, Inc.; 3 (BL) ©Nigel Cattlin/Holt Studios, (BC) Neg./Transparency no. K13073. Courtesy Dept. of Library Services/American Museum of Natural History; 5 (CR) ©Stone/Getty Images, (Bkgd) ©John Warden/Index Stock Imagery; 6 ©John Warden/Index Stock Imagery; 7 (BR) ©Jim Steinberg/Photo Researchers, Inc., (TR) ©Photographer's Choice/Getty Images; 8 ©DK Images; 9 (CR, TR, BR) ©DK Images, (TC) Getty Images; 10 (R) Silver Burdett Ginn, (TL) Getty Images; 11 ©DK Images; 12 ©Lou Jacobs Jr./Grant Heilman Photography; 13 (TR) ©George Bernard/NHPA Limited, (TR) ©DK Images, (CR) ©TH Foto-Werbung/Photo Researchers, Inc., (TR) ©Niall Benvie/Corbis, (BR) ©The Garden Picture Library/Alamy Images; 14 (BL) ©Stone/Getty Images, (BR) ©Jeff Lepore/Photo Researchers, Inc., (TL) ©Peter Smithers/Corbis; 15 (BR) ©DK Images, (TL) Getty Images; 16 (B) ©Carolina Biological/Visuals Unlimited, (TL) Getty Images; 17 (CL) ©M & C Photography/Peter Arnold, Inc., (TR) ©Brad Mogen/Visuals Unlimited, (TC) ©Pat O'Hara/Corbis, (CR) ©Wally Eberhart/Visuals Unlimited, (BR) ©DK Images; 18 (BC) ©Darryl Torckler/Getty Images, (CC) ©Brian Gordon Green/NGS Image Collection, (BC) ©John Poutier/Maxx Images, Inc., (BC) ©Jorg & Petra Wegner/Animals Animals/Earth Scenes, (TL) ©DK Images; 19 (L) ©DK Images, (CR) ©Steve Bloom Images/Alamy Images; 21 (CL) ©DK Images, (CR) Nigel Cattlin/Holt Studios, (BC) ©Kenneth W. Fink/Photo Researchers, Inc., (BC) ©Nigel Cattlin/Photo Researchers, Inc.; 23 (TR) ©Dr. E. R. Degginger/Color-Pic, Inc., (CL) ©John Cancalosi/Peter Arnold, Inc., (TL) Neg./Transparency no. K13073. Courtesy Dept. of Library Services/American Museum of Natural History, (BR) ©David Muench/Muench

Photography, Inc, (CR) ©James L. Amos/Corbis; 24 (BL) ©The Natural History Museum, London, (BR, TL) ©DK Images; 26 ©Ed Young/Corbis; 28 (TR) ©Dennis MacDonald/PhotoEdit, (CR) ©Inga Spence/Visuals Unlimited, (CR) ©Steven Emery/Index Stock Imagery, (BR) ©Comstock Inc.; 31 (TL) ©DK Images, (TR) ©Kenneth W. Fink/Photo Researchers, Inc.; 32 (Bkgd) ©MSFC/NASA, (TL, BR) NASA; **Chapter 2:** 33 (B) ©Barbara Von Hoffmann/Animals Animals/Earth Scenes, (Bkgd) ©David Harrison/Index Stock Imagery; 34 (BL) ©David L. Shirk/Animals Animals/Earth Scenes, (T) ©Tom Brakefield/Corbis, (BR) ©Jeff L. Lepore/Photo Researchers, Inc.; 35 (BL, BR) ©Brad Mogen/Visuals Unlimited; 37 (C) ©David Stover/ImageState, (Bkgd) ©Tom Brakefield/Corbis, 38 ©Tom Brakefield/Corbis, 39 (BR) ©Tom Vezo/Nature Picture Library, (BC) ©Zefa/Masterfile Corporation, (BL) ©Taxi/Getty Images, (BC) ©Natural Visions/Alamy Images, (TR) ©Frans Lanting/Minden Pictures; 40 (B) ©Tom Brakefield/Bruce Coleman Inc., (TL) ©Randy M. Ury/Corbis; 41 (CR) ©DK Images, (BC) ©Jim Brandenburg/Minden Pictures, (BR) ©Frans Lanting/Minden Pictures, (CR) Getty Images, (TR) ©Ken Lucas/Visuals Unlimited; 42 (BL) Jupiter Images, (TL) ©David Aubrey/Corbis; 43 (TL) ©Danny Lehman/Corbis, (TR) ©Robert Pickett/Corbis, (CR) ©The Image Bank/Getty Images, (BR) ©Brian Rogers/Visuals Unlimited; 44 (TL, TR) ©DK Images, (BR) ©Charles Melton/Visuals Unlimited; 45 (B) ©Brad Mogen/Visuals Unlimited; 46 (TL) ©Dick Scott/Visuals Unlimited; 46 (CL) ©Bettmann/Corbis, (BL) ©Keren Su/China Span/Alamy Images, (TL) ©Zefa/Masterfile Corporation; 47 (TR) ©Carolina Biological Supply Company/Phototake, (CL, BL) ©DK Images, (TL) ©Breck P. Kent/Animals Animals/Earth Scenes, (BR) ©Randy M. Ury/Corbis; 48 (BR) ©DK Images, (BR) ©Ken Lucas/Visuals Unlimited, (TL) ©Tony Evans/Timelapse Library/Getty Images; 49 (CL) ©Frans Lanting/Minden Pictures, (TR) ©Kevin Schafer/Corbis, (CR) ©Gary W. Carter/Corbis, (BR) ©DK Images; 50 ©Vittoriano Rastelli/Corbis, (TL) ©Photodisc Green/Getty Images; 51 (TC) ©Rod Planck/Photo Researchers, Inc., (CC) ©James Robinson/Animals Animals/Earth Scenes, (TL) ©Michael Quinton/Minden Pictures, (TR) ©Chris Newbert/Minden Pictures, (CL) ©The Image Bank/Getty Images, (BL) ©Rolf Kopfle/Bruce Coleman Inc., (BC) ©Tim Laman/NGS Image Collection, (BC) ©Suzanne L. & Joseph T. Collins/Photo Researchers, Inc., (CC) ©Steve E. Ross/Photo Researchers, Inc., (TC) ©Ken Wilson/Papilio/Corbis, (CR) ©David Aubrey/Corbis, (BR) ©E. R. Degginger/Bruce Coleman, Inc., (BL) ©Rick & Nora Bowers/Visuals Unlimited; 52 (TR) ©DK Images, (CR) ©George Grall/NGS Image Collection, (BR) ©Jeff L. Lepore/Photo Researchers, Inc., (TL) ©Eric and David Hosking/Corbis, (TL) ©Photodisc Blue/Getty Images; 53 (T) ©Gerry Ellis/Minden Pictures, (B) ©Terry W. Eggers/Corbis; 54 (TL) ©James L. Amos/Photo Researchers, Inc., (B) ©DK Images, (CL) ©Layne Kennedy/Corbis; 55 (TL) ©DK Images, (TR) ©Breck P. Kent/Animals Animals/Earth Scenes; 56 (R) ©Breck P. Kent/Animals Animals/Earth Scenes, (B) Senekenberg Nature Museum/©DK Images, (TL) Colin Keates/Courtesy of the Natural History Museum, London/©DK Images; 57 ©Ross M. Horowitz/Getty Images; 58 ©Larry L. Miller/Photo Researchers, Inc.; 60 Digital Vision; 61 ©Masa Ushioda/Visual & Written/Bruce Coleman, Inc.; 63 ©DK Images; 64 (TL) ©Dutheil Didier/SYGMA/Corbis, (BL) ©Reuters/Corbis; **Chapter 3:** 65 (Bkgd) Getty Images, (T) ©Photodisc Green/Getty Images; 66 (T) ©Mark E. Gibson Stock Photography, (BL) ©J. Eastcott/Y. Eastcott Film/NGS Image Collection, (BR) ©Enzo & Paolo Ragazzini/

Corbis; 67 (BL) ©Andy Binns/Ecoscene, (BR) ©Jim Zipp/Photo Researchers, Inc., (CR) ©Alan Carey/Photo Researchers, Inc., (TR) ©Steve Kaufman/Corbis; 69 ©Mark E. Gibson Stock Photography; 70 ©Mark E. Gibson Stock Photography; 71 ©Siede Preis/Getty Images; 72 Getty Images; 73 (Bkgd) ©Melissa Farlow/Aurora & Quanta Productions, (TC) ©DK Images, (BC) ©Kurt Stier/Corbis; 74 (CL) ©Royalty-Free/Corbis, (BL) ©Alan Carey/Photo Researchers, Inc.; 75 (CR) ©Joseph Van Os/Getty Images, (L) ©Kennan Ward/Corbis, (BR) Darren Bennett/Animals Animals/Earth Scenes; 76 ©OSF/Animals Animals/Earth Scenes; 77 (T) ©Enzo & Paolo Ragazzini/Corbis, (BL) ©Jason Edwards/NGS Image Collection, (BR) ©Steve Kaufman/Corbis; 78 (BL) ©Jack Dykinga/Getty Images, (BR) Jerry Young/©DK Images, (TL) ©DK Images; 79 (Bkgd) ©J. Eastcott/Y. Eastcott Film/NGS Image Collection, (TL) Daniel J. Cox/Natural Exposures; 80 (BL) Daniel J. Cox/Natural Exposures, (TL) ©Ed Reschke/Peter Arnold, Inc.; 81 (L) ©Andy Binns/Ecoscene, (TR, CL, CR) Daniel J. Cox/Natural Exposures; 82 ©Tim Laman/NGS Image Collection; 83 (T) ©Michio Hoshino/Minden Pictures, (TL, BR) ©Jim Brandenburg/Minden Pictures, (BL) ©Jay Dickman/Corbis, (CR) ©David Ulmer/Stock Boston; 84 (CR) ©Roy Toft/NGS Image Collection, (TR) ©Claus Meyer/Minden Pictures, (BR) ©Ken Preston-Mafham/Animals Animals/Earth Scenes, (TL) Alamy; 85 (BL) ©Michael & Patricia Fogden/Minden Pictures, (TL) ©Tui De Roy/Minden Pictures; 86 (B) Daniel J. Cox/Natural Exposures, (TR) ©Jim Zipp/Photo Researchers, Inc., (TL) ©Roy Toft/NGS Image Collection; 87 (Bkgd) Daniel J. Cox/Natural Exposures, (TR) ©Joseph H. Bailey/NGS Image Collection; 88 (TL) ©Medford Taylor/NGS Image Collection, (BR) ©Fred Bavendam/Peter Arnold, Inc.; 89 (TR) ©Mick Turner/PhotoLibrary, (Bkgd) ©Royalty-Free/Corbis; 90 Getty Images; 95 ©Ken Preston-Mafham/Animals Animals/Earth Scenes; 96 ©Bettmann/Corbis; **Chapter 4:** 97 ©M. Colbeck/OSF/Animals Animals/Earth Scenes; 98 (T) ©Stephen Frink/Corbis, (BL) ©Carol Havens/Corbis, (BR) ©K. H. Haenel/Zefa/Masterfile Corporation; 99 (BL) ©D. Robert and Lorri Franz/Corbis, (TR) ©Jim Brandenburg/Minden Pictures, (CR) ©Dr. Gopal Murti/Photo Researchers, Inc., (BR) ©Gerald Hinde/ABPL/Animals Animals/Earth Scenes; 101 (CR) ©Richard Walters/Visuals Unlimited, (Bkgd) ©Stephen Frink/Corbis, (BR) ©Bob Marsh/Papilio/Corbis, (CC) ©David Boag/Alamy Images; 102 ©Stephen Frink/Corbis; 103 (CR) Brand X Pictures, (BR) ©Patti Murray/Earth Scenes/Maxx Images, Inc., (CR) ©Laura Sivell/Papilio/Corbis, (TR) Getty Images; 104 (B) ©Richard Kolar/Animals Animals/Earth Scenes, (T) ©Rick Raymond/Index Stock Imagery; 105 (T) ©Michael & Patricia Fogden/Corbis, (B) ©B. Jones/M. Shimlock/Photo Researchers, Inc.; 106 (BL) ©Chase Swift/Corbis, (BC) ©Carol Havens/Corbis, (BR) ©Frank Blackburn/Ecoscene/Corbis, (TL) ©Hope Ryden/NGS Image Collection; 107 (B) ©D. Robert and Lorri Franz/Corbis, (TL) ©K. H. Haenel/Zefa/Masterfile Corporation, (CL) ©Randy Wells/Corbis, (BL) ©Danny Lehman/Corbis; 108 (TL, BL) Getty Images, (BR) ©Yva Momatiuk/John Eastcott/Minden Pictures, (BC) ©Naturfoto Honal/Corbis, (CC) ©Kevin R. Morris/Corbis; 109 (CL) Minden Pictures, (R) ©Claudia Adams/Alamy Images, (BL) ©Tom Brakefield/Corbis; 110 (TL) ©Gerry Ellis/Minden Pictures, (CL) ©Michael & Patricia Fogden/Corbis, (BL) ©Martin Harvey/Photo Researchers, Inc., (TL) ©Photodisc Green/Getty Images; 111 ©Gerald Hinde/ABPL/Animals Animals/Earth Scenes; 112 (T) ©DK Images, (CL) ©Raymond Gehman/Corbis, (BL) ©Scott Camazine/Photo